Fast & Fresh
ENTERTAINING

Fast & Fresh
ENTERTAINING

Delicious recipes to make in under 30 minutes

Maddalena Bonino

KYLE CATHIE LIMITED

First published in Great Britain in 1994 by
Kyle Cathie Limited
7/8 Hatherley Street
London SW1P 2QT

ISBN 1 85626 130 1

A Cataloguing in Publication record for this title is
available from the British Library.

Food stylist Liz Trigg
Designed by Tamasin Cole
Printed and bound in Great Britain
by Butler and Tanner Limited, Frome, Somerset

Front cover photograph of *Tortiglioni with Asparagus & Sun-dried
Tomato Pesto* (page 33); back cover photograph of *Duck Breast with
Roasted Red Onion & Beetroot served with a Ginger Sauce* (page 55) and
Stir-fry of Cabbages with Indonesian Noodles & Peanuts (page 80)

Contents

To Nat

Introduction

I hope the title *Fast & Fresh* will not mislead any readers of this book into thinking the recipes it contains are 'fresh' versions of 'fast food'. The preparation of food should not be hurried, but with practice any cook will acquire speed, and with a few hints about timing, many a dish can be assembled in a short time. With that in mind most, if not all, the recipes in this book can be prepared in about 30 minutes, but don't be disappointed if it takes longer the first time you try one of the dishes.

Also, remember that a well-balanced meal does not need to be structured into three courses. When you have friends round make sure you can share their company and enjoy the food with them! Don't spend too much time worrying about shopping and cooking; simply ensure you use good, fresh ingredients, follow the recipes and have fun!

Unless otherwise stated, all the recipes are for four people.

SPICY RED LENTIL SOUP WITH PARSLEY & LEMON YOGHURT

Lentils with a difference. Red split lentils give this soup a wonderful 'creamy' texture. Delicious hot or warm.

50 g / 2 oz unsalted butter
2 tablespoons olive oil
1 medium onion, sliced
2 cloves of garlic, chopped
½ teaspoon ground cumin
½ teaspoon ground coriander
1 small bulb of fennel, sliced
50 g / 2 oz fresh ginger, peeled & grated
1 stick of lemon grass, sliced
1 small red chilli, de-seeded & chopped (optional)
1 litre / 1¾ pints hot vegetable stock or water
300 g / 10 oz red split lentils
salt & freshly ground black pepper
juice & grated rind of 1 lemon
1 tablespoon Greek-style yoghurt
1 tablespoon chopped flat-leaf parsley

1   Heat the butter and oil in a large saucepan. When they begin to sizzle, add the onion, garlic, cumin and coriander and fry for a couple of minutes. Then add the fennel, ginger, lemon grass and chilli, if used. Add half the stock or water and cook for 10 minutes.

2   Add the lentils and the remaining stock or water, season and simmer for a further 10–15 minutes. Add the lemon juice and liquidize in a blender.

3   In a small bowl mix the yoghurt and lemon rind with 1 tablespoon water. Add the parsley and season.

4   Serve the soup with a dollop of seasoned yoghurt, accompanied by warm naan bread or warm buttered pitta bread.

CHESTNUT, MUSHROOM & ROCKET SOUP

I'm sure the thought of cooking and peeling chestnuts may deter some people from trying this recipe. Fear not! You can find cooked and peeled chestnuts vacuum-packed in most supermarkets or good delicatessens!

350 g / 12 oz brown cap button mushrooms
50 g / 2 oz unsalted butter
2 tablespoons olive oil
1 medium onion, sliced
2 cloves of garlic, chopped
100 g / 4 oz chestnuts, cooked & peeled
1 litre / 1¾ pints hot vegetable stock or water
salt & freshly ground black pepper
2 tablespoons balsamic vinegar
50 g / 2 oz rocket leaves, cut into thin strips
1 tablespoon chopped flat-leaf parsley

1 Wash the mushrooms well and chop them roughly.

2 Heat two-thirds of the butter with the oil in a large saucepan. When they begin to sizzle, add the onion and garlic and fry for a few seconds. Then add the mushrooms and two-thirds of the chestnuts. Simmer for a couple of minutes, then add the stock or water.

3 Season and leave to cook for about 15 minutes.

4 Transfer to a food processor or liquidizer and whizz until smooth. Return to the pan and stir in the vinegar, rocket and parsley. Cover and keep hot.

5 Finely chop the remaining chestnuts. Melt the rest of the butter in a small pan and toss the chestnuts in it. Season well and fry until browned.

6 Serve the soup with the chopped chestnuts sprinkled on top, accompanied by crusty country bread.

COURGETTE & ROSEMARY SOUP WITH DITALINI PASTA

Ditalini is a pasta shape specially designed to be used in soups or broths. Look in any Italian deli for other such shapes.

100 g / 4 oz ditalini pasta (small thimbles)
salt and freshly ground black pepper
3 tablespoons olive oil
1 medium onion, finely diced
1 clove of garlic, finely chopped
2 sprigs of fresh rosemary, washed and leaves removed
1 litre / 1¾ pints hot vegetable stock or water
700 g / 1½ lb courgettes, washed and thinly sliced
50 g / 2 oz Parmesan cheese, freshly grated
2 tablespoons extra-virgin olive oil

1 First cook the pasta. Bring a large saucepan of salted water to the boil, drop in the ditalini and cook until just tender or *al dente*. Drain and rinse in cold water. Drain well again, then toss the pasta in 1 tablespoon of the olive oil to prevent it from sticking together. Set aside.

2 Heat the remaining olive oil in a large saucepan. Add the onion, garlic and rosemary and fry until the onion becomes transparent. Add in the stock or water and season well.

3 Bring to the boil, then drop in the courgettes. Return to the boil and cook for a couple of minutes, then add the cooked pasta.

4 Serve the soup sprinkled with the grated Parmesan and the extra-virgin olive oil.

CLEAR FISH SOUP WITH SQUID, PRAWNS & MUSSELS

A fragrant and refreshing soup. Try different combinations of fish and shellfish with the basic stock.

1 litre / 1¾ pints water
2 tablespoons soy sauce
2 tablespoons sake
1 teaspoon wasabi (Japanese horseradish)
2 sticks of lemon grass, thinly sliced
25 g / 1 oz fresh ginger, cut into thin strips
5 coriander stalks, leaves removed & reserved
1 small red chilli, seeds removed & cut into strips (optional)
20 mussels, shells scrubbed & 'beards' removed
100 g / 4 oz baby squid, cleaned & cut into thin strips
100 g / 4 oz prawns, cooked & peeled
1 red pepper, cut into thin strips
1 spring onion, thinly sliced
1 medium carrot, cut into thin strips
50 g / 2 oz fine bean shoots
salt & freshly ground black pepper

1 First make the stock. Bringing the water to the boil in a large saucepan with the soy sauce, sake, wasabi, lemon grass, ginger, coriander stalks and chilli, if used.

2 Cook the mussels: heat a heavy-based saucepan, and when hot put in the mussels and cover with a tight-fitting lid. Holding the lid down firmly, shake the pan two or three times. The intense heat will make the mussels spring open in a few minutes. When all the mussels are open, remove from the heat, drain and keep warm. Discard any that do not open.

3 Place the squid, prawns and cooked mussels in a large serving bowl or individual bowls with the pepper, spring onion, carrot and bean shoots. Season then pour the piping hot stock over, garnish with the reserved coriander leaves and ENJOY!

FRESH SWEETCORN, SUN-DRIED TOMATOES & SMOKED HADDOCK CHOWDER

Chowders usually combine meat and fish. In this case the sun-dried tomatoes substitute the meat.

Serves 6–8 as a soup, 4 as a meal

> *75 g / 3 oz unsalted butter*
> *1 medium bulb of fennel, sliced*
> *1 large potato, peeled & diced*
> *1 medium onion, sliced*
> *1 clove of garlic, chopped*
> *2 small leeks, sliced*
> *6 sun-dried tomatoes, thinly sliced*
> *100 g / 4 oz baby sweetcorn, sliced*
> *zest of 1 lemon, finely chopped*
> *1.4 litres / 2½ pints warm milk*
> *225 g / 8 oz smoked undyed haddock, skinned &*
> *   bones removed*
> *salt & freshly ground black pepper*
> *1 small red chilli, de-seeded & finely sliced (optional)*
> *3 tablespoons chopped flat-leaf parsley*

1   Melt the butter in a large saucepan. Add the fennel, potato and onion and simmer for a few minutes. Add the garlic, leeks, sun-dried tomatoes, sweetcorn and lemon zest.

2   Pour in the milk and bring to the boil. Skim, then simmer for about 10 minutes until the potatoes are soft.

3   Cut the haddock into rough pieces. Add to the pan, season with plenty of pepper and add the chilli, if used.

4   Return to the boil, skim again if necessary, and check the seasoning. Stir in the parsley, cover and leave to stand for 5 minutes. Serve the soup with toasted bread.

See photograph on page 17

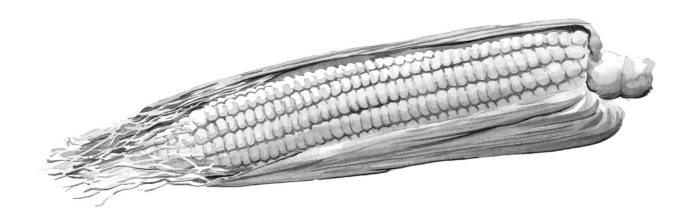

ONION SOUP WITH SMOKED CHICKEN & GRUYÈRE

A nice blend of strong flavours: more of a meal than a mere soup.

75 g / 3 oz butter
1 tablespoon olive oil
350 g / 12 oz onions, sliced
1 tablespoon brown sugar
1 tablespoon plain flour
1 teaspoon mustard powder
2 tablespoons dry white wine

2 tablespoons balsamic vinegar
1 litre / 1¾ pints hot chicken stock
225 g / 8 oz smoked chicken, boned & chopped
salt & freshly ground black pepper
75 g / 3 oz Gruyère cheese, grated
2 tablespoons flat-leaf parsley, chopped

1 Heat the butter with the oil in a large saucepan. When they begin to sizzle, add the onions and fry until soft.

2 Add the sugar and leave to caramelize for a minute or two, stirring occasionally. Sprinkle in the flour and mustard and cook for a couple of minutes, then add the wine, vinegar and stock, stirring well.

3 Add the chicken, bring to the boil and season. Cook for a further 5 minutes. Serve the soup sprinkled with the Gruyère, chopped parsley and freshly ground black pepper, accompanied by plenty of crusty French bread.

SAVOY CABBAGE, SMOKED PANCETTA & POTATO SOUP

Definitely a soup for a cold day. Pancetta is Italian bacon; but I prefer the spicing and curing treatment my compatriots give to this widely used ingredient.

2 tablespoons olive oil
150 g / 4 oz smoked pancetta or oak-smoked bacon
1 large potato, peeled & diced
1 medium onion, sliced
½ medium savoy cabbage, washed & cut into strips,
    stalks & ribs removed

zest of 1 orange, finely chopped
1 litre / 1¾ pints hot vegetable stock or water
salt & freshly ground black pepper
75 g / 3 oz mature Cheddar cheese, grated

1 Heat the oil in a large saucepan, then add the pancetta or bacon and leave to sizzle until almost crisp.

2 Add the potato and onion and fry briskly for a couple of minutes, then lower the heat and simmer for a further 5 minutes.

3 Add the cabbage, orange zest and stock or water. Bring to the boil, season and simmer for about 10 minutes until the potato is soft but the cabbage still slightly crunchy.

4 Serve the soup sprinkled with the grated Cheddar and freshly ground black pepper, accompanied by crusty bread.

TUSCAN BEAN SOUP WITH PESTO

Bean soups are delicious 'the day after', so if you have any left over try re-heating it in a warm oven in an ovenproof dish, drizzled with olive oil and covered with thin slices of onion. The Tuscans call this 'ribollita' (reboiled).

Serves 6–8 as a soup, 4 as a meal

2 tablespoons olive oil
50 g / 2 oz lean pancetta, cut into small cubes
1 medium onion, diced
clove of garlic, chopped
1 carrot, peeled & diced
2 sticks of celery, diced
1 medium leek, diced
75 g / 3 oz savoy cabbage, cut into thin strips
200 g / 7 oz cannellini beans, cooked, washed & drained

200 g / 7 oz borlotti beans, cooked, washed & drained
1 large ripe tomato, diced
1 sprig of fresh rosemary
1 sprig of fresh thyme
1.4 litres / 2½ pints hot vegetable stock or water
salt & freshly ground black pepper
4 slices of day-old country-style bread
1 clove of garlic, halved
4 tablespoons pesto (see below)

1   Heat the oil in a large saucepan. Add the pancetta and fry for a few minutes, then add the onion, chopped garlic, carrot, celery, leek and cabbage. Leave to sizzle for a couple of minutes, then add the beans, tomato and herbs. Add the stock or water and season.

2   Bring to the boil, then simmer for 15–20 minutes.

3   Meanwhile, toast the slices of bread and rub with the cut garlic. Place a slice at the bottom of each serving bowl, pour over the hot soup and serve with a dollop of pesto.

PESTO

100 g / 4 oz pine-nuts
2 cloves of garlic, peeled
a large bunch of basil
100 ml / 3½ fl.oz olive oil
100 ml / 3½ fl.oz extra-virgin olive oil
75 g / 3 oz Parmesan cheese, freshly grated
salt and freshly ground black pepper

1   Place the pine-nuts, garlic and basil in a food processor, and whizz to obtain a well-blended paste. Then pour in the two oils while the machine is still running. Scrape the pesto out of the processor and blend in the Parmesan. Check the seasoning and use as required.

NOTE: When you make pesto, make more than you need for the recipe. Pesto improves by 'standing' in the fridge. Just pour the excess into a jar, screw the lid on tightly and use when required.

Tuscan Bean Soup with Pesto,
and Fresh Sweetcorn, Sun-dried Tomatoes
& Smoked Haddock Chowder
(page 14)

VEGETABLE SOUP WITH BARLEY & CHORIZO SAUSAGE

Chorizo is a delicious Spanish spicy sausage that can be eaten raw or cooked, and it's not unlike the Neapolitan 'salamella'. It is possible that while the Spanish governed southern Italy in the fifteenth and sixteenth centuries they left behind not only laws and taxes but a few recipes as well!

2 tablespoons olive oil
170 g / 6 oz chorizo sausage, peeled and sliced
1 onion, peeled and diced
1 clove of garlic, chopped
1 carrot, peeled and diced
1 stick of celery, diced
1 small bulb of fennel, diced
1 courgette, diced
1 parsnip, peeled and diced

1 head of spring greens, sliced into strips
100 g / 4 oz pearl barley, soaked in warm water for 30 minutes
1 sprig of fresh thyme
3 bay leaves
1.4 litres / 2½ pints hot vegetable stock or water
salt and freshly ground black pepper
1 tablespoon chopped flat-leaf parsley

1 Heat the oil in a large saucepan. Add the chorizo, onion and garlic and fry for a couple of minutes, then add all the vegetables one at a time, stirring well between each addition. Finally add the drained barley, thyme and bay leaves.

2 Add the stock or water, season and bring to the boil. Skim, then simmer for about 15–20 minutes.

3 Serve the soup piping hot, sprinkled with the parsley and accompanied by toasted ciabatta bread rubbed with garlic.

ROAST TOMATO SOUP SERVED WITH CHOPPED OLIVES, PEPPERS & EGG

700 g / 1½ lb plum or firm beef tomatoes, washed and halved
1 medium red onion, roughly chopped
3 cloves of garlic, peeled
25 g / 1 oz fresh ginger, peeled and grated
1 small bulb of fennel, roughly chopped
3 tablespoons olive oil
salt and freshly ground black pepper
400 ml / 14 fl.oz hot vegetable stock or water
2 tablespoons balsamic vinegar

For the salsa
1 small red pepper, de-seeded and finely diced
8–10 basil leaves, chopped
1 hard-boiled egg, chopped
50 g / 2 oz black olives, chopped
2 tablespoons extra-virgin olive oil

1 Place the tomatoes, onion, garlic, ginger and fennel in a roasting pan. Sprinkle with the olive oil, season and place in a pre-heated oven at 220°C/425°F/Gas Mark 7 for about 20 minutes, tossing from time to time until the vegetables are tender.

2 Remove from the oven, add the stock or water, sprinkle with the vinegar and liquidize in a blender. Adjust the seasoning and keep warm.

3 In a bowl mix the pepper, basil, egg and olives with 1 tablespoon of the extra-virgin olive oil. Season.

4 Serve the soup drizzled with the remaining extra-virgin olive oil and accompanied by the salsa.

SALADS

FRENCH BEAN, PRAWN & AVOCADO SALAD

Don't be tempted to skip the sesame seeds, and make sure you toast them lightly (just golden) in a pan or in the oven: they are the 'secret ingredient' of this recipe.

Serves 4 people as a starter or 2 people as a main course

2 tablespoons sesame seeds
450 g / 1 lb French beans, topped, tailed & cut in half
juice & rind of 1 lemon
1 tablespoon balsamic vinegar
1 tablespoon ketjap manis (see page 48)

3 tablespoons extra-virgin olive oil
½ small chilli, de-seeded & finely chopped (optional)
salt & freshly ground black pepper
225 g / 8 oz Norwegian prawns
4 spring onions, thinly sliced
2 avocados, stoned, peeled and cut into small chunks

1   Toast the sesame seeds in a heavy-based frying pan over a medium heat, tossing frequently until golden. Set aside to cool.

2   Bring a saucepan of salted water to a brisk boil. Drop in the French beans, return to the boil and cook for a couple of minutes until tender. Drain and refresh under cold running water.

3   Meanwhile make the dressing: mix together the lemon juice and rind, the vinegar, manis and oil in a bowl. Add the chilli, if used. Whisk well with a fork and season.

4   Toss the well-drained beans, the prawns, spring onions and the avocado in the dressing. Serve sprinkled with the sesame seeds.

WARM SALAD OF BABY CORN, COURGETTES & BEAN SPROUTS

Tofu, or bean curd, is made from puréed soy beans that have been cooked, curdled and then pressed into cakes, usually square. Tofu is pure protein, rich in minerals and vitamins but extremely low in fat and cholesterol.

Serves 4 people as a starter or 2 people as a main course

100 g / 4 oz silken tofu
25 g / 1 oz fresh ginger, peeled
4–5 stalks of coriander
1 clove of garlic, peeled
1 small Thai chilli, de-seeded (optional)
1 tablespoon balsamic vinegar
1 teaspoon clear honey
juice of 1 lemon
2 tablespoons ketjap manis (see page 48)

2 tablespoons olive oil
salt & freshly ground black pepper
1½ tablespoons sesame oil
200 g / 7 oz baby sweetcorn, quartered
2 medium courgettes, cut into thin batons
1 medium red pepper, cut into thin strips
75 g / 3 oz bean sprouts, rinsed & drained
1 head of radicchio, thinly sliced
4 spring onions, thinly sliced

1   Make the dressing: combine the tofu, ginger, coriander stalks, garlic, chilli, vinegar, honey, lemon juice, ketjap manis and oil in a liquidizer and whizz until smooth. Season and if too thick dilute with a little water. Set aside.

2   Heat the sesame oil in a wok or large frying pan and toss in it the baby sweetcorn, courgettes, red pepper and bean sprouts. Season and stir-fry for a couple of minutes.

3   Prepare a base of radicchio on a serving plate. Spoon on the stir-fried vegetables, then the dressing, and serve sprinkled with the spring onions.

WARM SMOKED CHICKEN, RED ONION & SPINACH SALAD

You could also try this salad substituting the chicken with smoked quail, smoked mackerel or, even better, smoked eel.

Serves 4 people as a starter or 2 people as a main course

1 medium red onion, sliced
1 tablespoon soft brown sugar
3 tablespoons balsamic vinegar
3 tablespoons red wine vinegar
salt & freshly ground black pepper
1 teaspoon French mustard
2 tablespoons extra-virgin olive oil

3 tablespoons olive oil
300 g / 10 oz baby spinach leaves, washed & well drained
600 g / 1¼ lb smoked chicken, boned & roughly chopped
1 punnet of mustard & cress

1   First marinate the onion. In a bowl mix together the sugar, 1 tablespoon of the balsamic vinegar, the wine vinegar and a pinch of salt. Stir until the salt and sugar have dissolved, then add the onion. Toss well and leave to marinate for at least 20 minutes.

2   Make the dressing: mix together the mustard and the remaining balsamic vinegar in a bowl until well blended, then add the oils, whisking thoroughly with a fork or whisk. Season.

3   Dress the spinach with a couple of tablespoons of the dressing and toss well.

4   Place the chicken, the drained marinated onion and the remaining dressing in a frying pan and heat gently over a low flame, stirring frequently. When the dressing starts to simmer, remove from the heat. Spoon out on to the dressed spinach, sprinkle with the cress and serve. Boiled new potatoes would be a perfect accompaniment.

FENNEL, PEAR, PECAN NUT & DOLCELATTE SALAD

Dolcelatte is a deliciously mild creamy blue cheese produced in northern Italy. If you prefer a stronger cheese use Gorgonzola or a mature stilton.

Serves 4 people as a starter or 2 people as a main course

50 g / 2 oz pecan nuts, roughly chopped
2 medium bulbs of fennel, thinly sliced
juice of ½ lemon
30 g / 1 oz fresh ginger, peeled & cut into very fine strips or grated
1 tablespoon balsamic vinegar

3 tablespoons extra-virgin olive oil
salt & freshly ground black pepper
1 comice pear, ripe but firm, washed
225 g / 8 oz dolcelatte cheese, cut into small chunks
1 tablespoon finely chopped chives

1   Toast the pecan nuts in a pre-heated oven at 220°C/425°F/Gas Mark 7 for about 8–10 minutes until slightly darkened. Remove from the oven and leave to cool.

2   Toss the fennel with the lemon juice to prevent discoloration.

3   Make the dressing: mix the ginger, vinegar and oil in a bowl. Whisk with a fork and season.

4   Slice the pear and toss with the fennel, half the nuts and the dressing. Sprinkle with the dolcelatte, the remaining nuts, the chives and freshly ground black pepper. Serve accompanied with crusty bread or toasted sun-dried tomato ciabatta bread.

CHICK-PEA, SALT COD, ROASTED RED ONION & PARSLEY SALAD

You can find pre-soaked salt cod in some delicatessens, otherwise ask your fishmonger or make enquiries at the fish counter at the supermarket.

Serves 4 people as a starter or 2 people as a main course

4 small red onions
3–4 tablespoons extra-virgin olive oil
salt & freshly ground black pepper
300 ml/10 fl.oz milk
300 ml/10 fl.oz water
2 bay leaves
450 g/l lb salt cod, pre-soaked overnight
1½ tablespoons sherry vinegar
1 clove of garlic, finely chopped
1 teaspoon French mustard
1 tablespoon flat-leaf parsley
400 g/14 oz cooked chick-peas

1 Peel the onions and place them in a roasting pan with a little oil and seasoning. Bake in a pre-heated oven at 200°C/400°F/Gas Mark 6 for about 20 minutes. Remove from the oven and leave to cool slightly, then cut into segments.

2 While the onions are cooking, place the milk and water in a large saucepan with the bay leaves and bring to the boil. Add the well-drained salt cod and simmer for about 10–15 minutes, skimming the cooking liquor when necessary. Drain the salt cod well when cooked.

3 Meanwhile, make the dressing: mix together the oil, vinegar, garlic, mustard and half the parsley. Whisk well with a fork and season with plenty of freshly ground black pepper. Toss the chick-peas, onion segments and warm cod in the dressing. Serve sprinkled with the remaining parsley. If served as a main course, accompany with roast or baked potatoes.

CHICKEN, OYSTER MUSHROOM & FRISÉE SALAD
WITH PINE-NUTS & SULTANAS

Combining savoury flavours with sweet ones is a habit that goes back to Medieval times and the influence of the Moors in the Mediterranean, particularly in southern Spain and Italy.

Serves 4 people as a starter or 2 people as a main course

2 x 225-g / 8-oz chicken breasts, skinned
600 ml / 1 pint water
80 g / 3 oz unsalted butter
juice of 1 lemon
salt & freshly ground black pepper
100 g / 4 oz pine-nuts
350 g / 12 oz oyster mushrooms, stalks removed
100 g / 4 oz sultanas
1 teaspoon Dijon mustard
3 tablespoons extra-virgin olive oil
1½ tablespoons balsamic vinegar
1 small clove of garlic, finely chopped
1 tablespoon finely chopped chives
1 small head of frisée lettuce, washed & drained

1 First poach the chicken breasts. Bring the water to the boil in a saucepan and add one-third of the butter and half the lemon juice. Season, then add the chicken breasts and simmer for about 15 minutes. Turn off the heat and leave the chicken to cool in the cooking juices for 5–10 minutes, then remove and cut into strips.

2 Toast the pine-nuts on a baking tray in a pre-heated oven at 230°C/425°F/Gas Mark 8 for 5–10 minutes or until golden. Remove from the oven and leave to cool.

3 Melt the remaining butter in a frying pan and when it begins to sizzle, toss in the mushrooms and sultanas and season well. Remove from the heat and toss the mushrooms and sultanas with the chicken and pine-nuts in a bowl.

4 Make the dressing: mix the mustard, the remaining lemon juice, the oil, balsamic vinegar and garlic in a bowl. Whisk well with a fork and season. Toss the salad with the dressing, sprinkle with the chives and serve on a bed of frisée lettuce leaves. If served as a main course, accompany with boiled potatoes.

Chicken, Oyster Mushroom & Frisée Salad
with Pine-nuts & Sultanas,
and Warm Salad of Squid & Watercress
with Roasted Peanut Dressing
(page 26)

WARM SALAD OF SQUID & WATERCRESS WITH ROASTED PEANUT DRESSING

Look for blanched (skinless) unsalted peanuts in health shops or oriental grocers.

Serves 4 people as a starter or 2 people as a main course

> 100 g/4 oz unsalted peanuts
> salt & freshly ground black pepper
> 2 tablespoons white wine vinegar
> 2 tablespoons ketjap manis (see page 48)
> 1½ tablespoons sake
> 1 tablespoon balsamic vinegar
> ½ tablespoon honey
> 4 tablespoons extra-virgin olive oil
> ½ small red onion, diced
> 450 g/l lb small squid (12.5–15 cm/5–6 in), cleaned & cut into rings
> rind of 1 lemon
> 200 g/7 oz watercress, washed & drained
> 12 cherry tomatoes, halved

1 Toast the peanuts in a pre-heated oven at 230°C/450°F/Gas Mark 8 until evenly browned. Remove from the oven and leave to cool.

2 Bring a saucepan of salted water acidulated with the wine vinegar to the boil.

3 Meanwhile, make the dressing: in a bowl mix together the ketjap manis, sake, balsamic vinegar, honey, two-thirds of the extra-virgin olive oil and the onion. In a food processor coarsely grind the peanuts, then add to the dressing, mix well and season.

4 Drop the squid rings into the boiling water, return to the boil and immediately drain well. Toss the squid with the lemon rind and the remaining oil in a bowl.

5 To assemble the salad, mix the watercress and cherry tomatoes together, pile the warm squid on top and finally spoon on the peanut dressing.

See photograph on page 25

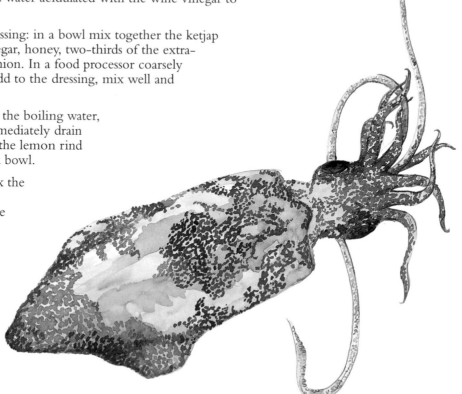

WARM SALAD OF POTATO, ROCKET & SMOKED MACKEREL WITH A HORSERADISH & RED ONION DRESSING

Serves 4 people as a starter or 2 people as a main course

450 g / 1 lb new potatoes, well-scrubbed & quartered
170 g / 6 oz creamed horseradish
½ small red onion, finely diced
3 tablespoons crème fraîche
juice of 1 lemon

3 tablespoons extra-virgin olive oil
1 tablespoon finely chopped flat-leaf parsley
salt & freshly ground black pepper
4 smoked mackerel fillets
100 g / 4 oz rocket leaves, washed & drained

1   Bring a saucepan of salted water to the boil, add the potatoes and simmer gently for 15–20 minutes until tender.

2   Meanwhile, make the dressing: mix together the horseradish, onion, crème fraîche, lemon juice, oil and parsley in a bowl. Whisk well with a fork, season and set aside.

3   Warm the mackerel fillets under the grill or in a pre-heated oven at 230°C/450°F/Gas Mark 8 for about 5 minutes, then flake roughly.

4   When the potatoes are cooked, drain well and toss in a bowl with the mackerel and the dressing. Arrange on a bed of rocket leaves and serve sprinkled with freshly ground black pepper.

LAMB'S LETTUCE, MARINATED ARTICHOKES & PARMA HAM SALAD WITH PARMESAN SHAVINGS

Marinated artichokes are readily available in good delicatessens and most supermarkets, but if you want to make your own I have given instructions in the note below.

Serves 4 people as a starter or 2 people as a main course

1 tablespoon sherry vinegar
1½ tablespoons hazelnut oil
2 tablespoons extra-virgin olive oil
salt & freshly ground black pepper
225 g / 8 oz lamb's lettuce, washed & drained

8 thin slices of Parma ham, cut into strips
4 marinated artichokes, cut into segments
2 plum tomatoes, cut into segments
100 g / 4 oz Parmesan cheese

1   Make the dressing: mix the vinegar and oils together in a bowl. Whisk well with a fork, and season.

2   Assemble on a serving plate the lamb's lettuce, Parma ham, artichokes and tomatoes. Sprinkle with the dressing. Using a potato peeler, shave the Parmesan directly on to the salad.

NOTE: To make your own marinated artichokes, take small firm fresh globe artichokes, peel back the outer leaves until you almost reach the core, trim the base and peel away the fibrous skin of the stalks. Cook in boiling salted water acidulated with lemon juice or white wine vinegar for 20–40 minutes or until a knife can easily pierce the base. Drain well and leave to cool. Remove the choke, then pack tightly into a jar with garlic, bay leaves, peppercorns and chilli. Cover with extra-virgin olive oil and seal. Keep in a cool dry place or in the fridge.

see photograph on page 28

COS LETTUCE, TUNA, QUAIL'S EGGS & ROASTED PLUM TOMATOES

The cooking of the tuna for this salad can be done in advance, and if you always found tinned tuna dry and tasteless maybe cooking the fish in this way will make you think again!

Serves 4 people as a starter or 2 people as a main course

>   4 x 100-g / 4-oz tuna steaks
>   3 cloves of garlic, chopped
>   1 sprig of fresh rosemary
>   1 stick of lemon grass, split in two
>   1 small red chilli, de-seeded & chopped (optional)
>   300 ml / 10 fl.oz olive oil
>   12 quail's eggs
>   4 firm plum tomatoes, halved
>   3 tablespoons extra-virgin olive oil
>   salt & freshly ground black pepper
>   3 tablespoons mayonnaise
>   1 tablespoon balsamic vinegar
>   juice of 1 lemon
>   1 tablespoon finely chopped flat-leaf parsley
>   1 small head of cos lettuce, washed, drained & cut into strips
>   3 spring onions, thinly sliced
>   2 lemons, halved, to serve

1   First cook the tuna. Place the steaks in a heavy-based frying pan with the garlic, rosemary, lemon grass and chilli, if used, and pour over the olive oil. Bring to simmering point over a low heat and cook for about 10 minutes. Remove from the heat and leave to cool in the oil.

2   Meanwhile, cook the quail's eggs. Place them in a pan of cold water, bring to the boil and cook for 1 minute, then drain immediately. Peel the eggs under cold running water, cut in half and set aside.

3   Place the tomatoes in a roasting pan, sprinkle with 1 tablespoon of the extra-virgin olive oil, salt and pepper and bake in a pre-heated oven at 230°C/450°F/Gas Mark 8 for 5–8 minutes. Remove from the oven and keep warm.

4   Make the dressing: mix the mayonnaise, vinegar, the remaining extra-virgin olive oil, lemon juice and parsley together in a bowl. Whisk well with a fork and season.

5   Toss the cos lettuce, spring onions and quail's eggs in the dressing. Add the roasted plum tomatoes and crumble the warm tuna over the top. Serve with lemon halves, accompanied by warm pitta bread.

Cos Lettuce, Tuna, Quail's Eggs
& Roasted Plum Tomatoes,
and Lamb's Lettuce, Marinated Artichokes
& Parma Ham Salad with Parmesan Shavings
(page 27)

BROCCOLI, CAULIFLOWER & ROASTED PEPPER SALAD
WITH ANCHOVY DRESSING

Anchovies are widely used in the Italian cooking repertoire both as an ingredient and a flavouring. Their preparation and preservation hasn't changed much since the days Roman matrons and fishmongers began layering the fresh fish with rock salt in small barrels.

Serves 4 people as a starter or 2 people as a main course

>   2 small yellow peppers
>   2 small red peppers
>   salt & freshly ground black pepper
>   225 g / 8 oz broccoli florets
>   225 g / 8 oz cauliflower florets
>   4 anchovy fillets in oil
>   2 tablespoons balsamic vinegar
>   juice of lemon
>   1 teaspoon English mustard
>   5 tablespoons olive oil
>   1 clove of garlic, peeled
>   1 teaspoon clear honey
>   1 tablespoon chopped flat-leaf parsley

1   Roast the peppers in a pre-heated oven at 230°C/450°F/Gas Mark 8 for about 15–20 minutes, or until the skins have blistered. Remove from the oven, place in a bowl and cover with cling-film. Leave to cool slightly, then skin, de-seed and cut the flesh into strips.

2   While the peppers are roasting, bring a saucepan of salted water to the boil. Drop in the broccoli, return to the boil and cook for 1 minute. Remove the broccoli with a perforated spoon and rinse under cold running water. Repeat this process for the cauliflower but this time cook for 3–4 minutes.

3   Make the dressing: place the anchovies, vinegar, lemon juice, mustard, oil, garlic and honey in a liquidizer and whizz until well blended. Adjust the seasoning and add a little water if the dressing is too thick. Toss the vegetables together in the dressing and serve sprinkled with the parsley, accompanied by bruschetta.

NOTE: Bruschetta is toasted ciabatta bread rubbed with garlic and sprinkled with extra-virgin olive oil (see page 78).

PASTA

TORTIGLIONI WITH ASPARAGUS & SUN-DRIED TOMATO PESTO

The Romans considered the asparagus an aphrodisiac: I'm sure they read more into the shape of this delicious vegetable than was necessary! Asparagus is at its best in Europe around May and June. If it is not available, substitute with mangetout.

salt & freshly ground black pepper
16–20 stems of asparagus, white base removed & stalks peeled
400 g / 14 oz tortiglioni (slightly twisted pasta tubes)

For the pesto
170 g / 6 oz sun-dried tomatoes
50 g / 2 oz whole almonds
2 cloves of garlic
75 g / 3 oz flat-leaf parsley, roughly chopped
zest of 1 lemon
100 ml / 3.5 fl.oz olive oil
100 ml / 3.5 fl.oz extra-virgin olive oil
50 g / 2 oz Parmesan cheese, freshly grated
salt & freshly ground black pepper

1 Bring a large saucepan of salted water to the boil. Add the asparagus and blanch for 1 minute, then remove from the water with a perforated spoon and refresh in cold water. Drain well and slice.

2 Return the cooking water to the boil and cook the tortiglioni.

3 Make the pesto: place the sun-dried tomatoes, almonds, garlic, parsley and lemon zest in a food processor and whizz until all the ingredients are well blended, then steadily pour in the two oils while the machine is still running. Remove the mixture from the food processor and place in a bowl. Stir in the Parmesan and check the seasoning.

4 When the pasta is cooked, take 1½ cups of the hot water and gently mix it into the pesto. Add the asparagus and the well-drained pasta, mix well and serve.

FETTUCCINE WITH SPINACH, MUSHROOM & GOAT'S CHEESE

Fresh goat's cheese (British or French) melted with crème fraîche makes a delicious creamy sauce for pasta, much tastier than double cream alone.

salt & freshly ground black pepper
100 g / 4 oz unsalted butter
2 shallots, finely chopped
1 clove of garlic, finely chopped
275 g / 10 oz chestnut button mushrooms, washed & sliced
juice of ½ lemon
2 tablespoons crème fraîche
100 g / 4 oz fresh goat's cheese, cut into small chunks
170 g / 6 oz fresh small-leaf or baby spinach, washed, drained & roughly chopped
400 g / 14 oz fettuccine (ribbon noodles)

1   Bring a large saucepan of salted water to the boil.

2   Meanwhile, melt the butter in a frying pan. When it begins to sizzle, add the shallots and garlic and leave to colour for a couple of minutes, then add the mushrooms and lemon juice. Season and cook until most of the juice has evaporated.

3   Spoon the crème fraîche and goat's cheese into the pan. Leave to simmer over a low heat, stirring occasionally, until the cheese has melted, then add the spinach and leave to wilt in the sauce.

4   Cook the fettuccine. When it is ready, drain well, then toss in the sauce and serve with a final sprinkling of freshly ground black pepper.

FARFALLE WITH FENNEL, SALMON & PINK PEPPERCORNS

Pink peppercorns have a delicate aromatic pip inside the pink shell, so when using ensure you grind them to a fine dust to make the most of their almost exotic perfume.

salt & freshly ground black pepper
1 large bulb of fennel, thinly sliced
400 g / 14 oz farfalle (pasta bows)
225 g / 8 oz mascarpone cheese
3 tablespoons crème fraîche
2 tablespoons dry white wine
1 tablespoon finely ground pink peppercorns
1 tablespoon finely chopped dill
2 tablespoons finely chopped chives
170 g / 6 oz smoked salmon, cut into strips

1 Bring a large saucepan of salted water to the boil. Add the fennel and blanch for 1 minute. Remove with a perforated spoon, refresh under cold running water and set aside. Keep the hot water to cook the farfalle in.

2 While the pasta cooks, make the sauce: in a large saucepan gently heat the mascarpone with the crème fraîche and the wine. Season, then add the fennel, the pink pepper and half the herbs.

3 When the pasta is ready drain well, toss in the sauce and lastly add the salmon strips. Serve immediately, sprinkled with the remaining herbs.

PENNE WITH MERGEZ SAUSAGES, RED ONION, TOMATOES & ROCKET

Mergez are spicy beef or lamb sausages, originating from Algeria. They are also very popular in France.

salt & freshly ground black pepper
400 g / 14 oz penne (pasta quills)
2 tablespoons olive oil
275 g / 10 oz mergez sausages, cut into bite-size pieces
1 red onion, thinly sliced
2 tablespoons dry white wine
12 cherry tomatoes, halved
75 g / 3 oz rocket leaves, thinly sliced
50 g / 2 oz Parmesan cheese, freshly grated

1 Bring a large saucepan of salted water to the boil and cook the penne.

2 Heat the oil in a large frying pan. Add the mergez sausage and the onion and fry for a couple of minutes. Add the wine and simmer for 8–10 minutes, then add the tomatoes.

3 When the pasta is ready, drain well and toss in the sauce with the rocket. Mix well, check the seasoning and serve with the Parmesan.

PIPE WITH AUBERGINES, FRESH TOMATO, BASIL & RICOTTA

Ricotta is a by-product of cheese-making, obtained by reheating the whey, and it varies in texture depending on the richness of the milk used. Look for delicate flavours and a creamy texture.

2 aubergines
salt & freshly ground black pepper
6 tablespoons olive oil
400 g / 14 oz pipe (pipe-shaped pasta)
1–2 tablespoons extra-virgin olive oil
1 medium red onion, finely chopped

1 clove of garlic, finely chopped
2 medium beef tomatoes, peeled & chopped
12 large basil leaves, roughly torn into pieces
225 g /8 oz ricotta, crumbled with a fork
4 tablespoons freshly grated Parmesan cheese

1   First prepare the aubergines. Cut them into cubes, sprinkle generously with salt and leave to drain for 20 minutes. Then wash off the salt and pat dry.

2   Heat a roasting pan with 3–4 tablespoons of the olive oil in a pre-heated oven at 230°C/450°F/Gas Mark 8 for a couple of minutes. When the oil is hot very carefully toss the cubes of aubergine in it and roast in the oven, stirring occasionally, for 10–15 minutes until golden and soft. Remove from the roasting pan and keep warm.

3   Meanwhile bring a large saucepan of salted water to the boil and cook the pipe.

4   While the pasta cooks, make the sauce: heat the remaining olive oil and the extra-virgin olive oil in a frying pan with the onion and garlic. Simmer for a couple of minutes, then add the tomatoes and seasoning. Cook for 5 minutes then add the aubergines.

5   When the pasta is ready, drain well and toss in the sauce. Lastly add the basil and sprinkle with the ricotta. Toss quickly but thoroughly and serve with a dusting of Parmesan.

FUSILLI WITH ROASTED PEPPERS, CAPERS & ANCHOVIES

Anchovies are often used in southern Italian cooking to enhance flavours. This type of sauce/dressing for pasta is usually served on the eve of religious celebrations which entail serious cooking – and serious eating – prior to a period of fasting.

2 red peppers
1 yellow pepper
2 tablespoons olive oil
400 g / 14 oz fusilli (pasta twists)
2 tablespoons extra-virgin olive oil
5–6 anchovy fillets

2 cloves of garlic, finely chopped
1 tablespoon balsamic vinegar
1 tablespoon small capers, washed & squeezed dry
1 tablespoon flat-leaf parsley, finely chopped
1 tablespoon toasted breadcrumbs

1   Place the peppers in a roasting pan, drizzle with a little of the olive oil and roast in a pre-heated oven at 230°C/450°F/Gas Mark 8 for 15–20 minutes, or until most of the skins have blistered. Remove from the oven, place in a bowl, cover with cling-film and leave to cool slightly, then peel and cut the flesh into strips.

2   Bring a large saucepan of salted water to the boil and cook the fusilli.

3   Meanwhile, heat the two oils in a large frying pan with the anchovies and the garlic over a medium to low heat, stirring gently. When the anchovies dissolve into the sauce, add the vinegar, capers and the pepper strips.

4   When the pasta is ready, drain well and toss in the sauce with the parsley. Serve sprinkled with the breadcrumbs.

SPAGHETTI WITH SMOKED DUCK, SPRING ONIONS & CHILLI

Try to find Spaghetti alla Chitarra for this dish – most well-known brands produce them. The Chitarra is a wooden rectangular frame with steel wires stretched across it. The rolled-out sheet of fresh pasta is pressed through the wires with a rolling pin to produce square spaghetti.

salt
400 g / 14 oz spaghetti
3 tablespoons olive oil
1 red pepper, de-seeded & cut into thin strips
1–2 small red chillies, de-seeded & diced
1 clove of garlic, sliced
100 g / 4 oz pak choy (Chinese spinach), washed & thinly sliced
170 g / 6 oz smoked duck, sliced
1 tablespoon balsamic vinegar
1½ tablespoons ketjap manis (see page 48)
4 spring onions, sliced

1 Bring a large saucepan of salted water to the boil and cook the spaghetti.

2 Heat the oil in a wok or large frying pan, add the pepper, chilli (use 2 if you like the dish hot), garlic and pak choy and stir-fry for a couple of minutes over a high heat.

3 Add the duck, vinegar and ketjap manis. When the pasta is ready, drain well and stir into the sauce with the spring onions. Toss well and serve. Chopsticks are optional!

CONCHIGLIE WITH MUSSELS, COURGETTES & OLIVES

This recipe calls for a tin of chopped plum tomatoes as I find it very difficult to buy ripe and flavoursome fresh plum tomatoes at market stalls or supermarkets. But if you have better luck than me, do use fresh ones.

450 g / 1 lb fresh mussels, shells scrubbed & 'beards' removed
salt & freshly ground black pepper
3 tablespoons olive oil
1 medium onion, chopped
1 clove of garlic, finely chopped
2 medium courgettes, cut into bite-size pieces
1 x 400-g / 14-oz tin of chopped plum tomatoes
juice of 1 lemon
10 black olives, sliced
10 green olives, sliced
400 g / 14 oz conchiglie (pasta shells)
2 tablespoons chopped flat-leaf parsley
2 tablespoons extra-virgin olive oil

1   First cook the mussels: heat a heavy-based saucepan and when hot, put in the mussels and cover with a tight-fitting lid. Cook for about 5–10 minutes, shaking the pot vigorously, while holding the lid down firmly. When all the mussels have opened, remove from the heat and drain in a colander. Discard any that do not open.

2   Bring a large saucepan of salted water to the boil.

3   Shell the mussels, keeping some in the shell to garnish.

4   Heat the olive oil in a large frying pan. Add the onion and garlic and fry for a couple of minutes, then add the courgettes. Cook over a medium to high heat until golden, then add the chopped tomatoes and simmer for 10 minutes. Add the mussels, lemon juice, olives and seasoning.

5   Meanwhile, cook the conchiglie in the boiling water. When it is ready, drain well and toss in the sauce. Serve sprinkled with the parsley and the extra-virgin olive oil drizzled over.

GARGANELLI WITH LEEKS & SCALLOPS IN A SAFFRON SAUCE

Scallops are my favourite shellfish. When buying them, make sure they are fresh (firm flesh almost translucent), and do not overcook them as you may lose their flavour and sensual texture.

salt & freshly ground black pepper
3 leeks, sliced, washed & drained
400 g / 14 oz garganelli (hand-rolled pasta quills)
2 tablespoons dry white wine
½ teaspoon saffron strands

300 ml / 10 fl.oz double cream
3 tablespoons crème fraîche
grated rind of 1 lemon
1½ tablespoons finely chopped dill
12 king scallops

1 Bring a large saucepan of salted water to the boil. Blanch the leeks in it for 1 minute, then remove with a perforated spoon, refresh under cold running water and set aside.

2 Return to the boil and cook the garganelli.

3 Meanwhile, make the sauce: heat the wine with the saffron in a heavy-based frying pan and simmer until the liquid has reduced by half, then add the cream, crème fraîche, lemon rind and seasoning. Simmer for 3–4 minutes, then add the dill and leeks.

4 When the pasta is ready, drain well and toss in the sauce. While you toss the pasta, heat a dry frying pan over a high heat. Arrange the pasta on individual serving plates and sear the well-seasoned scallops in the hot frying pan for a minute or so on each side. Place on top of the prepared pasta and enjoy.

NOTE: If the scallops are very 'meaty', i.e. more than 2.5 cm/1 in thick, cut in half horizontally and proceed as instructed.

TAGLIOLINI WITH CRAB MEAT, SHALLOTS, LEMON GRASS & GINGER

East meets West: an almost typical cream sauce for a long-shaped pasta, given a slight edge with delicate and fresh oriental spicing.

salt & freshly ground black pepper
2 tablespoons olive oil
2 shallots, finely chopped
1 stick of lemon grass, finely chopped
50 g / 2 oz fresh ginger, peeled & grated
100 g / 4 oz brown crab meat
6 sun-dried tomatoes, cut into thin strips

juice of 1 lemon
2 tablespoons double cream
3 tablespoons crème fraîche
400 g / 14 oz tagliolini
170 g / 6 oz white crab meat
3 tablespoons chopped coriander leaves

1 Bring a large saucepan of salted water to the boil for the pasta.

2 Meanwhile, make the sauce: heat the oil in a frying pan, add the shallots, lemon grass and ginger and fry gently for a couple of minutes, then add the brown crab meat, sun-dried tomatoes and lemon juice and simmer for a minute or two. Add the cream, crème fraîche and seasoning.

3 While the tagliolini cooks, add the white crab meat and some of the coriander leaves to the sauce.

4 When the pasta is ready, drain well and toss in the sauce. Serve garnished with the remaining coriander leaves.

TORCHIETTI WITH BROCCOLI, DOLCELATTE SAUCE & PECAN NUTS

Torchietti is one of the many dozens of pasta shapes produced. Experiment with different shapes as you will find that one sauce often compliments a specific shape better than another.

salt & freshly ground black pepper
450 g / 1 lb broccoli florets
150 g / 5 oz mascarpone cheese
200 g / 7 oz dolcelatte cheese, cut into cubes
2 tablespoons crème fraîche
1 tablespoon balsamic vinegar
1 tablespoon dry white wine
400 g / 14 oz torchietti (twisted pasta curls)
50 g / 2 oz pecan nuts

1 Bring a large saucepan of salted water to the boil. Blanch the broccoli in it for 1 minute, then remove with a perforated spoon, refresh under cold running water and set aside. Keep the hot water to cook the torchietti in.

2 In a heavy-based saucepan gently heat the mascarpone and dolcelatte cheese with the crème fraîche, vinegar and wine until well blended. Season.

3 Cook the pasta and when it is ready, drain well.

4 Bring the sauce to simmering point and add the broccoli. Toss the pasta in the sauce and serve sprinkled with the pecan nuts and plenty of freshly ground black pepper.

GRILLED CHICKEN ESCALOPES
WITH AROMATIC COUS COUS & YOGHURT DRESSING

Cous cous is made from the ground core of the durum wheat grain and is the staple diet of most north African countries.

200 g / 7 oz cous cous
200 ml / 7 fl.oz boiling water
2 tablespoons extra-virgin olive oil
2 tablespoons finely chopped flat-leaf parsley
1 tablespoon finely chopped coriander
1 tablespoon finely chopped dill
1 tablespoon finely chopped chives
1 medium red onion, thinly sliced
1 medium red pepper, de-seeded & finely diced
salt & freshly ground black pepper
4 x 225-g / 8-oz chicken breasts, split in half horizontally

For the yoghurt dressing
4 tablespoons Greek strained yoghurt
1 clove of garlic, finely chopped
1 tablespoon extra-virgin olive oil
juice of 1 lemon
salt & freshly ground black pepper

1 First make the dressing by mixing together all the ingredients. Cover and set aside.

2 Prepare the cous cous: pour the hot salted water over the cous cous in a mixing bowl and leave to stand for 3–4 minutes until all the water has been absorbed. Add the oil, herbs, onion and pepper and keep stirring with a fork or metal spoon until all the ingredients are well mixed but the cous cous grains are separated. Check the seasoning and set aside.

3 Heat a grilling pan. Season the chicken escalopes and when the pan is hot, grill for 4–5 minutes on each side or until done.

4 Arrange the grilled escalopes on the cous cous and serve with the yoghurt dressing.

MEDALLIONS OF PORK IN SPICY COATING
WITH A WARM SALAD OF CRISPY VEGETABLES

Amongst the ingredients for this recipe you will find ketjap manis, a sweet thick Indonesian soy sauce. Use sparingly in marinades, sauces and dressings for a light oriental flavouring.

100 g / 4 oz plain flour
1 teaspoon ground cumin
½ teaspoon ground coriander
salt & freshly ground black pepper
170 g / 6 oz breadcrumbs
3 tablespoons sesame seeds
1 egg
2 tablespoons water
2–3 pork tenderloins, weighing in total about 600 g / 1¼ lb,
*   cut into thick slices & lightly beaten into medallions*
5 tablespoons olive oil
1 tablespoon ketjap manis
1 tablespoon balsamic vinegar
2 tablespoons extra-virgin olive oil
1 clove of garlic, finely chopped
50 g / 2 oz fresh ginger, peeled & grated
5 spring onions, thinly sliced
1 red pepper, de-seeded & cut into batons
1 yellow pepper, de-seeded & cut into batons
170 g / 6 oz mangetout, topped & tailed
75 g / 3 oz unsalted butter

1 Mix the flour with the cumin, coriander and seasoning. Mix the breadcrumbs with the sesame seeds. Whisk the egg with the water.

2 Toss the pork medallions in the seasoned flour, then dip in the egg wash, lastly coat with the breadcrumbs. Set aside.

3 Heat two tablespoons of the olive oil in a wok or large frying pan. While the oil heats up, mix together in a large bowl the ketjap manis, vinegar, extra-virgin olive oil, garlic, ginger and spring onions, and season. When the oil in the wok is almost smoking, carefully toss in the peppers and mangetout and stir-fry for a couple of minutes. Then tip into the prepared dressing in the bowl, mix well and set aside.

4 Heat the remaining oil with the butter in a large frying pan. When the butter begins to foam, fry the medallions for 3–4 minutes on each side.

5 Serve the medallions with the prepared vegetables. Rice or noodles would make a suitable accompaniment.

RAGOÛT OF RABBIT, LEEKS & GREEN LENTILS WITH WHOLEGRAIN MUSTARD

Rabbit meat is not a favourite in the British repertoire, which is a pity as it is tastier than most chicken and low in cholesterol.

200 g / 7 oz green lentils, previously soaked for 10–15 minutes
1 tablespoon plain flour
salt & freshly ground black pepper
700 g / 1½ lb rabbit, boned & cut into small chunks
50 g / 2 oz unsalted butter
2 tablespoons olive oil
2–3 leeks, sliced, washed & drained
1 clove of garlic, finely chopped
2 tablespoons wholegrain mustard
2–3 tablespoons dry white wine
150 ml / 5 fl.oz hot chicken stock or water
1 tablespoon balsamic vinegar
150 ml / 5 fl.oz double cream
1 tablespoon chopped flat-leaf parsley

1   Bring a saucepan of water to the boil. Drain the lentils and cook for 15–20 minutes until just soft.

2   Meanwhile, start to prepare the ragoût. Season the flour and toss the rabbit pieces in it. Shake off any excess.

3   Heat the butter with the oil in a large saucepan. When the butter begins to foam, add the rabbit, leeks and garlic and fry for a couple of minutes. Then add the mustard, wine and stock or water. Season, then simmer for 8–10 minutes.

4   When the lentils are ready, drain well. Add to the cooked ragoût and mix thoroughly. Add the vinegar and cream, check the seasoning and lastly stir in the parsley.

5   Serve with crusty bread or steamed new potatoes and a crisp salad.

See photograph on page 53

GRILLED LIVER ON A BED OF ROCKET LEAVES

Balsamic vinegar is obtained from ageing cooked concentrated must (grape juice) for seven to fifty or more years. The juice is kept in barrels or kegs made from different woods. As it ages the must thickens into a precious flavour-enhancing ingredient.

1½ medium red onions, finely diced
2 plum tomatoes, quartered, de-seeded & diced
1 tablespoon finely chopped chives
4 tablespoons extra-virgin olive oil
2 tablespoons balsamic vinegar
salt & freshly ground black pepper
450 g / 1 lb calves' liver, sliced
150 g / 5 oz rocket leaves, washed & drained

1   Make the salsa: in a bowl combine the onion, tomato, chives, oil and vinegar. Mix well and season. Set aside.

2   Season the liver. Heat a grilling pan and when the pan is very hot, grill the liver slices on both sides to your preferred taste.

3   Arrange the grilled liver on the rocket leaves (the heat of the liver will wilt the salad slightly) and spoon on the salsa. Serve with a warm potato salad.

SAUTÉ OF CHICKEN LIVERS & SHALLOTS ON SAGE POLENTA

The Romans cooked polenta made with a lesser kind of wheat and served it with meat stews. When Caesar's troops invaded Britain they brought the recipe with them but began to use a local grain – oats – leaving the Britons the tradition of porridge!

1 tablespoon olive oil
80 g / 3 oz butter
4 shallots, sliced
225 g / 8 oz button mushrooms, sliced
650 g / 1½ lb chicken livers
1 tablespoon red wine
1½ tablespoons balsamic vinegar
salt & freshly ground black pepper

For the polenta
1.2 litres / 2¼ pints milk
75 g / 3 oz butter
1 clove of garlic, finely chopped
6 sage leaves, finely sliced
salt & freshly ground black pepper
250 g / 9 oz instant polenta

1   First make the polenta: heat the milk in a saucepan with the butter, garlic, sage and seasoning. When it comes to the boil, lower the heat and pour in the polenta, stirring continuously. Cook, still stirring, for 1–2 minutes, then remove from the heat and keep warm. (The instructions on the packet will require less liquid, but for soft polenta follow this method. The photograph shows the alternative hard polenta which has been grilled.)

2   Heat the oil and half the butter in a large frying pan. When the butter begins to foam, add the shallots and mushrooms and cook over a high heat for a couple of minutes. Remove the mushrooms and shallots with a perforated spoon and keep warm.

3   Bring the fat in the pan to sizzling point again and toss in the chicken livers, searing well on all sides. Return the vegetables to the frying pan, add the wine and vinegar and cook for a couple of minutes. Season and blend in the remaining butter. Spoon the polenta on to a serving dish, making a well in the centre. Arrange the livers with their sauce in the well and serve.

LAMB CUTLETS ON A WARM TOMATO & ARTICHOKE SALAD

Choose well-trimmed cutlets with dark red meat, unless you are buying new season lamb.

12 lamb cutlets
salt & freshly ground black pepper
1 tablespoon olive oil
50 g / 2 oz unsalted butter
1 sprig of fresh rosemary
4 marinated artichokes, cut into segments (see page 27)
1 clove of garlic, finely chopped
4 plum tomatoes, quartered, de-seeded & cut into segments
150 g / 5 oz spinach leaves washed, drained & roughly chopped

1   Season the cutlets.

2   Heat the oil and butter with the rosemary in a large frying pan. When the butter begins to foam, sear the cutlets on both sides. Remove them from the pan with the rosemary and arrange on a baking tray. Cook in a pre-heated oven at 220°C/425°F/Gas Mark 7 for 5–6 minutes or longer if you prefer your lamb not quite pink.

3   Meanwhile, return the frying pan to the heat and bring back to sizzling point. Add the artichokes, garlic and tomatoes and quickly toss in the cooking juices. Add the spinach and warm through, checking the seasoning.

4   Distribute the warm salad on individual serving dishes and arrange the cutlets on top. Serve with baked potatoes or buttered basmati rice. Do not accompany with mint sauce!

Ragoût of Rabbit, Leeks & Green
Lentils (page 49), and Lamb Cutlets on
a Warm Tomato & Artichoke Salad

ESCALOPES OF VEAL ON ROASTED FIELD MUSHROOMS & WILTED SPINACH SERVED WITH ANCHOVY BUTTER

Blending different fresh herbs or flavourings with butter is an easy way to preserve perfumes and essences. A slice of flavoured butter can turn plain grilled meat or fish into an interesting meal.

150 g / 5 oz soft unsalted butter
6 anchovy fillets in oil, drained & chopped to a pulp
juice of ½ lemon
salt & freshly ground black pepper
4 large flat field mushrooms, stalks removed
2 tablespoons olive oil
50 g / 2 oz cold butter
1 small clove of garlic, finely chopped
400 g / 14 oz spinach leaves, washed, stalks removed & roughly chopped
4 x 200-g / 7-oz veal escalopes

1 First make the anchovy butter: using a wooden spoon blend together in a bowl the soft butter, anchovy pulp and lemon juice. Season, mix well and refrigerate.

2 Place the mushrooms in a roasting pan. Sprinkle with the oil and season. Bake in a pre-heated oven at 220°C/425°F/Gas Mark 8 for 15–20 minutes or until soft right through.

3 Remove the mushrooms from the oven and slice. Melt the cold butter in the roasting pan with the garlic, add the spinach and allow to wilt then add the sliced mushrooms and mix well.

4 While the mushrooms and spinach are cooking, heat a grilling pan. Season the veal escalopes and grill for a minute or so on each side.

5 Serve the veal arranged on the vegetables, with a curl of anchovy butter on each serving.

DUCK BREAST WITH ROASTED RED ONION & BEETROOT
SERVED WITH A GINGER SAUCE

When using duck breast try not to overcook the meat, for the more you cook it the tougher it will become. Before slicing and serving allow a few minutes 'resting' time – the meat will remain pink, tender and juicy.

1 tablespoon olive oil
4 red onions, peeled & cut into segments
4 raw beetroots, peeled & cut into segments
salt & freshly ground black pepper
100 ml/3⅓ fl.oz red wine
4 x 170-g /6-oz duck breasts, skin scored, patted dry & rubbed with salt
50 g /2 oz fresh ginger, peeled & cut into thin strips
2 tablespoons balsamic vinegar
80 g /3 oz unsalted butter, cut into small cubes

1   Heat the oil in a roasting pan. Add the onions and beetroot, season and moisten with a couple of spoonfuls of the wine. Cover with foil and bake in a pre-heated oven at 220°C/425°F/Gas Mark 7 for 15–20 minutes.

2   When the vegetables are half-way through their cooking, heat a frying pan and when it is hot, sear the duck breasts skin-side down for a couple of minutes, then turn over and cook for a further minute or two. Transfer to a baking tray and cook in the oven for a further 6–8 minutes, turning occasionally.

3   Remove the duck breasts from the oven and keep warm.

4   Remove the pan with the vegetables, place on the stove and remove the foil. Turn the heat up and add the ginger, remaining red wine and vinegar to the pan. Cook for a couple of minutes, then remove the vegetables and keep warm.

5   Let the juices in the pan reduce slightly, then gradually work in the butter, stirring continuously so that all the ingredients are well blended.

6   Place the beetroot and onions on a serving plate, slice the duck and arrange on the vegetables. Spoon around the sauce and serve.

ROASTED QUAILS on SPICED BASMATI RICE
with a SHERRY VINEGAR SAUCE

Quails are deliciously tasty and quick to cook. To enjoy them best – use your hands. (Fingerbowls essential!)

3 tablespoons olive oil
100 g / 4 oz unsalted butter
8 quails, washed & patted dry
salt & freshly ground black pepper
150 g / 5 oz basmati rice, washed & drained
2 shallots, finely sliced
1 teaspoon ground coriander seeds
½ cinnamon stick, crushed
1 small red pepper, de-seeded & finely diced
1 small red chilli, de-seeded & finely diced
2 tablespoons sherry vinegar
3 tablespoons crème fraîche
coriander leaves, to garnish

1 Heat 2 tablespoons of the oil with 25 g/1 oz of the butter in a roasting pan. When the butter begins to foam fry the quails on all sides until golden. Season and roast in a pre-heated oven at 220°C/425°F/Gas Mark 7 for about 15 minutes, turning the birds occasionally.

2 Meanwhile, prepare the rice: bring a large saucepan of salted water to the boil and cook the rice for about 10 minutes, until just tender. When it is ready, drain well, rinse under cold running water and set aside.

3 Heat the remaining oil and butter in a frying pan. When they begin to sizzle, add the shallots, coriander, cinnamon, pepper and chilli. Fry for a couple of minutes, then add the rice and mix well. Check the seasoning and keep warm.

4 Remove the cooked quails from the roasting pan and keep warm. Drain any excess fat from the roasting pan and place the pan over a high heat. Deglaze with the vinegar and leave to simmer and reduce for a minute or so. Then stir in the crème fraîche, check the seasoning and cook for a couple of minutes, to thicken.

5 Place the rice on serving plates, arrange the quails on top, spoon over the sauce and garnish with the coriander leaves.

NOTE: The sherry sauce may need to be passed through a sieve.

GRILLED SIRLOIN STEAK WITH PEPPERS, AUBERGINES & SALSA VERDE

This tasty relish is a classic northern Italian recipe traditionally served with boiled meats. I find it quite suitable for grills as well.

1 large aubergine
salt & freshly ground black pepper
5 tablespoons olive oil
2 red peppers, de-seeded & quartered
2 yellow peppers, de-seeded & quartered
2–3 cloves of garlic, crushed
4 x 200-g / 7-oz sirloin steak

For the salsa verde
1 bunch of flat-leaf parsley
50 g / 2 oz day-old bread, crusts removed
100 g / 4 oz gherkins, well drained
100 g / 4 oz capers, squeezed dry
4 anchovy fillets
2 cloves of garlic
5 tablespoons extra-virgin olive oil
salt & freshly ground black pepper

1   First prepare the aubergine. Cut in half lengthways, then crossways into thin segments. Sprinkle generously with salt and leave to drain for 20 minutes.

2   Heat two-thirds of the oil in a roasting pan. Wash the aubergine to remove the salt, pat dry and add to the pan. Season.

3   Heat the remaining oil in a second roasting pan and add the peppers and garlic. Season. Roast both pans of vegetables in a pre-heated oven at 230°C/450°F/Gas Mark 8 for about 15 minutes, tossing occasionally.

4   Meanwhile, make the salsa by blending all the ingredients in a food processor. Check the seasoning and set aside.

5   Heat a grilling pan. Season the steaks and when the pan is hot, grill them to your preferred taste.

6   Serve the steaks with the hot vegetables and the salsa verde. New potatoes or a crisp salad and crusty bread would complete this dish perfectly.

BAKED MACKEREL WITH CARROT NOODLES & ORANGE & CORIANDER DRESSING

This beautifully shiny fish has a high oil content which makes it ideal for grilling and baking.

4 large carrots
4 x 225-g /8-oz mackerel fillets
salt & freshly ground black pepper
1 teaspoon coriander seeds, crushed
2 shallots, finely diced
zest of 1 orange, grated
2 tablespoons fresh coriander leaves, finely chopped
1 tablespoon balsamic vinegar
2 tablespoons extra-virgin olive oil

1   Using a potato peeler, shave the carrots into 'noodles'.

2   Season the mackerel fillets with salt, pepper and the crushed coriander seeds. Place on a baking tray skin–side up and bake in a pre-heated oven at 230°C/450°F/Gas Mark 8 for 10 minutes.

3   Meanwhile, bring a saucepan of salted water to the boil and blanch the carrot noodles for a couple of seconds, then refresh under cold running water and drain well.

4   In a bowl mix together the shallots, orange zest, coriander leaves, vinegar, oil and seasoning.

5   When the fish is ready, arrange the noodles on a serving plate and season with a little of the dressing. Place the fish fillets on top, spoon over the remaining dressing and serve.

BAKED COD FILLETS WITH ROASTED LEEKS & HERB MAYONNAISE

Cod was once one of the most widely caught fishes, bought salted and dried. However, as the fishing grounds have been depleted fresh cod has become dearer and its culinary merits rediscovered.

4 tablespoons olive oil
25 g / 1 oz unsalted butter
4 x 170-g / 6-oz cod fillets
salt and freshly ground black pepper
75 g / 3 oz plain flour
4 medium leeks, sliced & washed

For the mayonnaise
3 egg yolks
2 teaspoons Dijon mustard
1½ tablespoons white wine vinegar
400 ml / 14 fl.oz olive oil
1 tablespoon finely chopped flat-leaf parsley
1 tablespoon finely chopped chives
1 tablespoon finely chopped dill
1 tablespoon chervil leaves
juice of 1 lemon
salt & freshly ground black pepper

1   Heat 1 tablespoon of the oil with the butter in a roasting pan. Dust the cod fillets with the seasoned flour, shaking off any excess. Fry the dusted fillets in the hot fat until golden on both sides.

2   Heat the remaining oil in a second roasting pan, add the leeks and cook over a high heat for a couple of minutes, then season. Cook the fish and leeks in a pre-heated oven at 220°C/425°F/Gas Mark 7 for about 10 minutes.

3   Meanwhile, prepare the mayonnaise: in a food processor blend together the egg yolks, mustard and vinegar, then add the oil in a steady stream, with the machine still running. When the mixture is well blended, spoon into a bowl and add the herbs, lemon juice and seasoning. Set aside.

4   When the fish and leeks are ready, arrange on serving plates and serve accompanied by the mayonnaise.

SAUTÉ OF SQUID, PRAWNS, MANGETOUT & BABY SWEETCORN WITH GARLIC & LEMON

Squid can be found in all the oceans and seas except the Black Sea. As far as cooking is concerned, it is most popular with oriental and Mediterranean cooks.

2 tablespoons olive oil
225 g / 8 oz squid, cleaned, cut into strips & well drained
225 g / 8 oz prawns, cooked & peeled
2 cloves of garlic, finely chopped
2 sun-dried tomatoes, cut into thin strips
150 g / 5 oz mangetout, topped, tailed & cut in half
150 g / 5 oz baby sweetcorn, quartered
juice & grated rind of 1 lemon
salt & freshly ground black pepper
1 tablespoon toasted sesame seeds

1 Heat the oil in a wok or large frying pan until it is almost smoking. Carefully toss in the squid and prawns and stir-fry for a couple of minutes.

2 Add the garlic, sun-dried tomatoes, mangetout and sweetcorn. Keep cooking over a high heat for a further 2 minutes, then add the lemon juice and rind.

3 Check the seasoning, sprinkle with sesame seeds and serve.

GRILLED PINK TROUT FILLET ON A HERB SALAD WITH MARINATED MUSHROOMS

Substitute the trout in the recipe with lemon sole fillets, brill or turbot for different contrasts of textures.

150 g / 5 oz brown button mushrooms, stalks removed & finely sliced
1 red onion, finely diced
1 small clove of garlic, finely chopped
1 tablespoon chopped flat-leaf parsley
juice & rind of 1 lemon
salt & freshly ground black pepper
3 tablespoons extra-virgin olive oil
150 g / 5 oz mixed lettuce leaves (preferably small ones)
6 chives, cut into 5-cm / 2-in pieces
2 tablespoons chervil leaves
1 sprig of lemon thyme, leaves removed
2 tablespoons flat-leaf parsley leaves
4 x 170-g / 6-oz pink trout fillets, skin removed

1 Place the mushrooms in a bowl with the onion, garlic, chopped parsley, lemon juice and rind. Season well and stir in the oil. Cover and leave to stand.

2 Toss the lettuce leaves with the herbs and set aside in a salad bowl.

3 Heat a grilling pan and when it is hot, sear the seasoned fish fillets for 2–3 minutes on each side (longer if you like your fish well done).

4 Arrange some salad on individual serving dishes, place the cooked fish on top and spoon on the marinated mushrooms. Buttered rice or new potatoes would make a suitable accompaniment.

Grilled Pink Trout Fillet on a Herb Salad with Marinated Mushrooms, and Roasted Monkfish with Grilled Courgettes & a Black Olive & Pine-nut Relish (page 66)

ROASTED MONKFISH *WITH* GRILLED COURGETTES *& A* BLACK OLIVE *&* PINE-NUT RELISH

Monkfish is a seriously ugly fish with a head almost twice the size of its body. The skinned tails are the most commonly eaten part, and some fishmongers sell the cheeks as a delicacy.

4 tablespoons olive oil
4 x 225-g / 8-oz monkfish tails, skinned
salt & freshly ground black pepper
3 medium courgettes, cut into thin diagonal slices
zest of 1 lemon, finely chopped
2 tablespoons extra-virgin olive oil
2 tablespoons flat-leaf parsley

For the relish
100 g / 4 oz black olives, rinsed & well drained
100 g / 4 oz pine-nuts, lightly roasted
1 clove of garlic
75 g / 3 oz flat-leaf parsley leaves
juice of 1 lemon
3 tablespoons olive oil
salt & freshly ground black pepper

1   First make the relish by blending all the ingredients in a food processor. Check the seasoning and set aside.

2   Heat a couple of tablespoons of olive oil in a roasting pan and sear the monkfish. Season and cook in a pre-heated oven at 220°C/425°F/Gas Mark 7 for 15–20 minutes.

3   Meanwhile, heat a grilling pan and when it is hot, grill the courgette slices, a few at a time. As you cook them, toss them into a bowl with the lemon zest, oils, parsley and seasoning.

4   When the monkfish is ready, serve with a mound of marinated courgettes and a spoonful of relish.

See photograph on page 64

POACHED FILLETS OF LEMON SOLE ON A RICE SALAD WITH ROASTED PEPPER SALSA

Rice and fish can be a wonderful combination. In this case the rice offers a contrasting texture to the fish and is a perfect foil for the salsa.

salt & freshly ground black pepper
200 g / 7 oz basmati rice, washed
1 tablespoon small capers, rinsed & squeezed dry
3 tablespoons finely chopped chives
2 small plum tomatoes, de-seeded & finely chopped
3 tablespoons extra-virgin olive oil
50 g / 2 oz unsalted butter
6 x 150-g / 5-oz lemon sole fillets, halved lengthwise

For the salsa
2 medium red peppers
1 medium yellow pepper
½ red onion, thinly sliced
3 tablespoons extra-virgin olive oil
1 tablespoon balsamic vinegar
salt & freshly ground black pepper

1   Place the peppers on a baking tray and bake in a pre-heated oven at 240°C/450°F/Gas Mark 8 for 15–20 minutes, turning occasionally. Remove from the oven and leave to cool.

2   Meanwhile, bring a saucepan of salted water to the boil and cook the rice. When ready, drain and refresh under cold running water. Toss the rice into a bowl with the capers, chives, tomatoes, oil and seasoning. Mix well and set aside.

3   Place on the stove a frying pan with high sides and half fill it with water. Add the butter and some seasoning and bring to a simmer. Fold the sole fillets in half and poach in the liquid over a low heat for about 8–10 minutes.

4   Meanwhile, peel the peppers, cut into small dice and mix with the onion, oil, vinegar and seasoning.

5   When the fish is ready, spoon the rice on to a serving dish, arrange the fish fillets on top, spoon over the salsa and serve.

ROASTED JOHN DORY WITH ROASTED TOMATO & OLIVE SALSA

John Dory is also known as St Peter's fish. The 'Fisher of Men' is said to have picked out a specimen from the day's catch to throw back into the sea, leaving the imprints of his thumb on one side of the fish and his forefinger on the other. To this day the silver-grey fish bears the marks on its skin.

2 tablespoons olive oil
25 g / 1 oz unsalted butter
4 x 170-g / 6-oz John Dory fillets
4–6 plum tomatoes, quartered
salt & freshly ground black pepper
2 tablespoons extra-virgin olive oil
2 lemons, halved

For the salsa
75 g / 3 oz black olives, pitted, rinsed,
    drained & chopped
75 g / 3 oz green olives, pitted, rinsed,
    drained & chopped
1 clove of garlic, finely chopped
1 red onion, finely chopped
3 tablespoons chopped flat-leaf parsley
1 tablespoon balsamic vinegar
2 tablespoons extra-virgin olive oil
salt & freshly ground black pepper

1   Heat the olive oil and butter in a roasting pan and fry the John Dory fillets, browning them on both sides. Add in the tomatoes, season and bake in a pre-heated oven at 220°C/425°F/Gas Mark 7 for about 8–10 minutes.

2   Meanwhile, prepare the salsa by mixing together all the ingredients.

3   Serve the fish with the softened tomato quarters, a spoonful of the salsa and a drizzle of extra-virgin olive oil, accompanied by lemon halves.

GRILLED TUNA STEAKS WITH A FENNEL, POTATO & TOMATO SALAD

Tuna are exceptionally fast swimmers as they need plenty of oxygen. When they swim at high speeds (up to 40 miles per hour) oxygenated water runs over their gills allowing them to breathe. All this swimming produces the powerful muscles which characterize tuna flesh.

salt & freshly ground black pepper
300 g / 10 oz firkin or new potatoes
4–5 tablespoons extra-virgin olive oil
1 medium bulb of fennel, sliced
1 medium red onion, thinly sliced

1 tablespoon finely chopped flat-leaf parsley
juice of 1 lemon
1 tablespoon balsamic vinegar
4 plum tomatoes, cut into segments
4 x 200-g / 7-oz tuna steaks

1   Bring a saucepan of salted water to the boil and cook the potatoes.

2   Meanwhile, heat 2 tablespoons of the oil in a frying pan, add the sliced fennel and stir-fry for a couple of minutes. Season and set aside. In a bowl mix together the onion, parsley, remaining oil, lemon juice and vinegar.

3   When the potatoes are cooked drain and refresh under cold running water for a couple of minutes, then while still warm quarter and toss in the prepared dressing with the fennel and tomatoes. Toss gently but thoroughly and set aside.

4   Heat a grilling pan and when it is hot, cook the seasoned tuna steaks to your preferred taste. Serve with the still warm salad and a little more extra-virgin olive oil, if necessary.

SEARED SALMON ESCALOPES ON A WATERCRESS, SUN-DRIED TOMATO & SPRING ONION SALAD WITH BASIL OIL

Salmon belongs to the northern hemisphere (Atlantic and Pacific oceans) and is one of its better known fish.

4 tablespoons extra-virgin olive oil
12–15 large basil leaves
salt & freshly ground black pepper
150 g / 5 oz watercress, washed & drained
6 sun-dried tomatoes, cut into thin strips
4 spring onions, thinly sliced
4 x 200-g / 7-oz salmon escalopes
2 lemons, halved

1 Blend the oil and basil with a pinch of salt in a liquidizer and set aside.

2 In a bowl toss together the watercress, sun-dried tomatoes, spring onions and a little of the basil oil.

3 Heat a dry, heavy-based frying pan until very hot, then sear the seasoned salmon escalopes for 3–4 minutes on each side if you like your salmon slightly rare in the middle, or a little longer to cook through.

4 Arrange the salad on individual serving plates, top with the salmon, sprinkle with the basil oil and serve with half a lemon.

BAKED SARDINES SERVED ON ROCKET LEAVES WITH AVOCADO & MARINATED RED ONION

Sardines are one of my favourite fish. They are full of flavour and must be bought very fresh because, like all oily fish, the flesh spoils quickly.

1 tablespoon brown sugar
1 tablespoon balsamic vinegar
2–3 tablespoons red wine vinegar
salt & freshly ground black pepper
1 red onion, thinly sliced
12 sardines gutted, heads removed & well washed to remove all the scales
2 small avocados
150 g / 5 oz rocket leaves, washed & drained

For the dressing
1 teaspoon mustard
3 tablespoons extra-virgin olive oil
1 tablespoon white wine vinegar
salt & freshly ground black pepper

1 First marinate the onion: in a bowl stir together the sugar, balsamic vinegar, red wine vinegar and a pinch of salt. When the salt and sugar have dissolved, add the onion. Toss well and leave to marinate for 20 minutes.

2 Place the sardines on a baking tray and season. Bake in a pre-heated oven at 220°C/425°F/Gas Mark 7 for about 10 minutes.

3 Make the dressing by blending the ingredients in a bowl with a fork. Set aside.

4 When the fish is ready, peel, stone and slice the avocados. Toss the rocket leaves with slices of avocado and the drained marinated onions. Place the salad on individual serving plates and arrange the fish on top. Sprinkle with the dressing and serve.

VEGETARIAN

GRILLED BEEF TOMATOES WITH BLACK OLIVE, FETA CHEESE & CHIVE TOPPING

Feta is traditionally made with ewe's milk and sometimes goat's milk. It should be lightly salty in flavour and crumbly in texture.

225 g / 8 oz feta cheese, grated
100 g / 4 oz black olives, washed, pitted & roughly chopped
1 tablespoon finely chopped chives
1 clove of garlic, finely chopped
1 tablespoon dry breadcrumbs
4 tablespoons extra-virgin olive oil
salt & freshly ground black pepper
4 large beef tomatoes, halved
1 tablespoon olive oil
100 g / 4 oz rocket leaves, to serve

1   In a bowl mix the feta with the olives, chives, garlic, breadcrumbs, 3 tablespoons of the extra-virgin olive oil and plenty of freshly ground black pepper. Sprinkle on to the cut side of the tomatoes, trying to cover the whole surface as neatly as possible.

2   Grease a baking tray with the olive oil and arrange the prepared tomatoes on it. Bake at 220°C/425°F/Gas Mark 7 for about 10 minutes until the topping is golden and the tomatoes heated through but still firm.

3   When the tomatoes are ready, serve on rocket leaves arranged on individual serving plates and drizzle over the remaining extra-virgin olive oil.

Grilled Beef Tomatoes with Black Olive,
Feta Cheese & Chive Topping,
and Baked Aubergines with Goat's
Cheese Mayonnaise (page 75)

BAKED FIELD MUSHROOMS WITH RICOTTA, PINE-NUTS & BASIL FILLING

Flat field mushrooms are commonly seen as the poor relation of wild mushrooms, probably because they are so easy to grow. If you know where to pick or buy wild flat field mushrooms make use of them instead.

250 g / 9 oz ricotta cheese
2 tablespoons extra-virgin olive oil
75 g / 3 oz pine-nuts, toasted
1 small clove of garlic, finely chopped
12 large basil leaves, chopped
salt & freshly ground black pepper
12 medium flat field mushrooms, stalks removed
1 tablespoon olive oil

For the dressing
2 plum tomatoes, quartered, de-seeded & diced
½ red onion, diced
1 tablespoon balsamic vinegar
salt & freshly ground black pepper

1 In a bowl mix the ricotta with half the extra-virgin olive oil, the pine-nuts, garlic, basil and seasoning. (The mixture should be moist and creamy; add 1–2 tablespoons of cream if necessary.)

2 Spoon the mixture on to the dark gills side of the mushrooms, pressing lightly to make it stick.

3 Grease a baking tray with the olive oil and arrange the stuffed mushrooms on it. Bake in a pre-heated oven at 220°C/425°F/Gas Mark 7 for about 15 minutes or until the mushrooms are soft through to the middle.

4 Meanwhile, prepare a dressing by mixing the tomatoes in a bowl with the onion, the remaining extra-virgin olive oil, the vinegar and seasoning.

5 When the mushrooms are ready, arrange on individual serving plates and serve with the dressing.

FENNEL, SUN-DRIED TOMATO, GOAT'S CHEESE & PINE-NUT GRATIN

Fennel is a delicious vegetable: serve it raw, thinly sliced in salad; steamed drizzled with extra-virgin olive oil, balsamic vinegar and Parmesan shavings; or braised with a little white wine for serving with fish, chicken or veal. It has good digestive properties.

salt & freshly ground black pepper
4 medium bulbs of fennel, cut into thin segments
25 g / 1 oz soft unsalted butter
75 g / 3 oz pine-nuts, lightly toasted

8 sun-dried tomatoes, cut into thin strips
1 bunch of chives, finely chopped
325 g / 11 oz fresh goat's cheese, crumbled

1 Bring a saucepan of salted water to the boil and blanch the fennel for 1 minute, then drain well.

2 Grease an ovenproof dish (or 4 individual ones) with the soft butter and arrange the fennel in it. Sprinkle on some pine-nuts, some sun-dried tomatoes, some chives and some of the goat's cheese. Season.

3 Repeat the operation until all the ingredients are used up (no more than 3 layers). Then bake in a pre-heated oven at 220°C/425°F/Gas Mark 7 for about 15 minutes or until the cheese topping is melted and crisp. Serve hot with a crisp salad and ripe tomatoes.

BAKED AUBERGINES WITH GOAT'S CHEESE MAYONNAISE

Aubergines are a favourite of mine but they haven't always been popular – they were once said to cause indecent behaviour in men and even be responsible for signs of madness! Luckily we have grown wiser as far as this extremely versatile vegetable is concerned.

2 large aubergines
salt & freshly ground black pepper
6–8 tablespoons olive oil
2–3 whole cloves of garlic, lightly crushed
150 g / 5 oz mixed salad leaves, washed & drained

For the mayonnaise
150 g / 5 oz fresh goat's cheese, cold, crumbled
1 tablespoon wholegrain mustard
1 tablespoon white wine vinegar
1 tablespoon olive oil
2 tablespoons extra-virgin olive oil
grated rind & juice of ½ lemon
1 bunch of chives, finely chopped

1 Cut the aubergines in half lengthways, then crossways into segments. Sprinkle generously with salt and leave to drain for 20 minutes. Wash to remove the salt and pat dry.

2 Divide the oil between 2 roasting pans and heat until almost smoking, then very carefully toss in the aubergine and garlic. Bake in a pre-heated oven at 220°C/425°F/Gas Mark 7 for 15–20 minutes, tossing occasionally, until the aubergines are golden and soft through.

3 Meanwhile, make the mayonnaise: place the goat's cheese, mustard and vinegar in a food processor and whizz until well amalgamated, then pour in both the oils in a steady stream with the machine still running. Remove the mayonnaise from the food processor and stir in the lemon rind and juice, chives and seasoning. Mix well and chill until ready to use.

4 When the aubergines are ready remove from the oven and arrange on the prepared salad leaves, on individual serving plates, discarding the garlic. Season with freshly ground black pepper and spoon on the mayonnaise.

See photograph on page 72

COURGETTE, RICOTTA & BASIL TIMBALE

For this recipe use aluminium dariole or timbale moulds as the heat will spread faster than if using glass or ceramic ramekins.

250 g / 9 oz ricotta cheese
1 egg
3 tablespoons extra-virgin olive oil
3 courgettes, washed & grated
12–16 basil leaves, chopped
50 g / 2 oz Parmesan cheese, grated
salt & freshly ground black pepper
4 tablespoons dry breadcrumbs
25 g / 1 oz soft butter

For the salsa
6 plum tomatoes, quartered, de-seeded & diced
1 bunch of chives, finely chopped
1 tablespoon balsamic vinegar
3 tablespoons extra-virgin olive oil
salt & freshly ground black pepper

1 In a bowl whisk the ricotta with the egg and oil until well blended. Then fold in the courgettes, basil, Parmesan, seasoning and half the breadcrumbs.

2 Grease 4 individual dariole moulds with the butter and dust with the remaining breadcrumbs.

3 Spoon the mixture into the moulds. Place on a baking tray and cook in a pre-heated oven at 200°C/400°F/ Gas Mark 6 for about 20 minutes.

4 Meanwhile, prepare the salsa by mixing together all the ingredients. Set aside.

5 When the timbales are ready, remove from the oven, unmould carefully on to individual serving plates and serve with the salsa.

ROAST VEGETABLES WITH TAHINI DRESSING

Tahini paste is obtained by crushing sesame seeds. It is delicious as a dip for raw or roast vegetables, as prepared in this recipe, but can also be served with plain grilled meat and fish. You can even try mixing it with the puréed flesh of roasted aubergines: a traditional Middle Eastern recipe.

4 tablespoons olive oil
1 bulb of fennel, cut into segments
2 red peppers, de-seeded & quartered
2 yellow peppers, de-seeded & quartered
1 red onion, cut into segments
1 leek, sliced
1 courgette, sliced
100 g / 4 oz baby sweetcorn, halved
1 medium carrot, peeled & sliced
8 shitake mushrooms, stalks removed
4 plum tomatoes, halved
salt & freshly ground black pepper

For the tahini dressing
3 tablespoons tahini paste
½ tablespoon clear honey
50 ml / 2 fl.oz extra-virgin olive oil
2 cloves of garlic, peeled
60 ml / 3 fl.oz water
4–5 sprigs flat-leaf parsley
salt & freshly ground black pepper
½ red chilli, de-seeded (optional)

1 Heat the oil in two baking trays. When hot, carefully toss in the vegetables and stir thoroughly. Season and roast in a pre-heated oven at 240°C/450°F/Gas Mark 8 for 10–15 minutes, stirring occasionally.

2 Meanwhile, prepare the dressing by blending all the ingredients in a liquidizer. Check the seasoning and set aside.

3 When the vegetables are ready, arrange on individual serving plates, drizzle over the dressing and serve. A crisp salad, rice or cous cous would make this a complete meal.

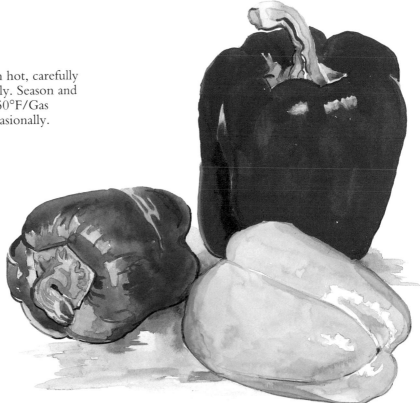

SPINACH, OYSTER MUSHROOM & TOMATO BRUSCHETTA WITH PARMESAN SHAVINGS & TRUFFLE OIL

Bruschetta is essentially a slice of toasted or grilled bread rubbed with a fresh clove of garlic and drizzled with extra-virgin olive oil. You can then embellish it with tomato, basil, anchovies, ricotta, or whatever you wish.

2 tablespoons olive oil
50 g / 2 oz unsalted butter
400 g / 14 oz oyster mushrooms, stalks removed
1 clove of garlic, finely chopped
450 g / 1 lb spinach, washed, drained & roughly chopped
2 plum tomatoes, cut into segments
salt & freshly ground black pepper
100 g / 4 oz Parmesan cheese
2 tablespoons truffle oil

For the bruschetta
1 loaf of ciabatta bread, sliced
1 clove of garlic, halved

1   Make the bruschetta by toasting the ciabatta bread slices and then rubbing them while still hot with the garlic clove. Arrange on individual serving plates.

2   Heat the olive oil with the butter in a large frying pan until foaming, then add the mushrooms and garlic and fry briskly until the juices in the pan are clear. Quickly add the spinach and allow to wilt, then fold in the tomatoes. Check the seasoning, then pile on to the bruschetta.

3   Using a potato peeler, shave the Parmesan on to the spinach and mushroom mixture, drizzle on the truffle oil and enjoy.

POTATO, ONION & PEPPER RAGOÛT WITH SAFFRON & MASCARPONE

Saffron is obtained by picking the stigmas of crocus flowers and drying them – a labour-intensive activity which accounts for the costliness of this wonderful spice.

50 g / 2 oz unsalted butter
1 tablespoon olive oil
225 g / 8 oz pearl onions, peeled
450 g / 1 lb potatoes, peeled & cut into small cubes
1 clove of garlic, finely chopped
12 saffron strands
2 tablespoons dry white wine

1 tablespoon balsamic vinegar
2 red peppers, de-seeded & sliced
2 yellow peppers, de-seeded & sliced
225 g / 8 oz mascarpone cheese
salt & freshly ground black pepper
2–3 tablespoons finely chopped flat-leaf parsley

1   Heat the butter and oil in a flameproof casserole. When they begin to foam, add the onions, potatoes, garlic and saffron strands. Fry for a few minutes, then add the wine and vinegar. Leave to evaporate for about a minute, then add the peppers and the mascarpone and mix well. Season.

2   Lower the heat, cover the casserole with a lid and simmer for 10 minutes.

3   Remove the lid, turn up the heat and cook for a further 5–8 minutes, stirring from time to time, until the juices are thick and creamy. Fold in the parsley and serve with cous cous or rice.

STIR-FRY OF CABBAGES WITH INDONESIAN NOODLES & PEANUTS

Oil noodles can be found already cooked in most Asian supermarkets. If you cannot find them, use dry Chinese noodles which are sold in most supermarkets.

3 tablespoons olive oil
100 g / 4 oz red cabbage, thinly sliced
100 g / 4 oz savoy cabbage, thinly sliced
100 g / 4 oz pak choy, thinly sliced
3 anchovy fillets (optional)
1 clove of garlic, finely chopped
1 medium red onion, thinly sliced
1 red pepper, de-seeded & thinly sliced

450 g / 1 lb Indonesian oil noodles
100 g / 4 oz Chinese cabbage, thinly sliced
1 small red chilli, de-seeded & finely chopped
  (optional)
2 tablespoons ketjap manis (see page 48)
salt & freshly ground black pepper
150 g / 5 oz peanuts, toasted & roughly chopped

1   Heat the oil in a wok or large frying pan until smoking. Carefully toss in the red cabbage, savoy cabbage, the sliced stalks of the pak choy, the anchovies, if used, and the garlic and stir-fry for a minute or two. Then add the onion and red pepper and stir-fry for a further couple of minutes.

2   Lastly add the noodles, Chinese cabbage, leaves of the pak choy, chilli and ketjap manis. Toss for a further minute or two until the noodles are heated through, check the seasoning and serve sprinkled with the peanuts.

NOTE: When stir-frying don't be tempted to add more oil if the ingredients seem too dry. Instead, add 1 tablespoon of water which will quickly evaporate: the steam produced will help cook the ingredients without burning them.

STEAMED BROCCOLI FLORETS ON GRILLED POLENTA WITH DOLCELATTE SAUCE

Polenta, as we know it, was first cooked in the Veneto region of Italy. The ships coming from the Americas unloaded their cargoes, which included maize, in Venice and the popularity of this ingredient quickly spread throughout northern Italy.

200 g / 7 oz dolcelatte cheese, cut into small chunks
150 g / 5 oz mascarpone cheese
1 tablespoon balsamic vinegar
2 tablespoons dry white wine
salt & freshly ground black pepper
700 g / 1½ lb broccoli florets
2 spring onions, thinly sliced

For the polenta
500 ml / 19 fl.oz water
500 ml / 19 fl.oz milk
2 tablespoons extra-virgin olive oil & a little extra for
  oiling
1 clove of garlic, finely chopped
salt & freshly ground black pepper
250 g / 9 oz instant polenta
50 g / 2 oz pecan nuts, toasted & finely chopped

1 First make the polenta by bringing the water, milk, oil, garlic and seasoning to the boil in a saucepan. Pour in the polenta in a steady stream, stirring continuously. Cook for 5 minutes over a low heat, add the pecan nuts and stir well. Remove from the heat and spread on a lightly oiled baking tray. Leave to set in a cool place for about 20 minutes.

2 Place the dolcelatte, mascarpone, vinegar, white wine and seasoning in a saucepan and heat gently until melted.

3 Meanwhile, bring a saucepan of salted water to the boil and heat a grilling pan. When the water boils, cook the broccoli for a couple of minutes (longer if you prefer your vegetables less crunchy), then drain and keep warm.

4 Cut the polenta into quarters and grill for a couple of minutes on both sides.

5 Place the grilled polenta on individual serving plates, arrange the broccoli on top and spoon over the sauce. Sprinkle with the spring onion and freshly ground black pepper.

AMARETTI & RASPBERRY CUSTARD

Amaretti are traditional biscuits from Piedmont and Lombardy, made with a mixture of sweet and bitter almonds.

Serves 4–5

> 600 ml/1 pint double cream
> 1 teaspoon vanilla essence or 1 vanilla pod, split in half lengthways
> 6 egg yolks
> 100 g/4 oz caster sugar
> 1 tablespoon marsala wine
> 170 g/6 oz fresh raspberries
> 6 amaretti biscuits, crushed

1 In a small heavy saucepan gently heat the cream with the vanilla essence or pod.

2 Meanwhile, whisk the yolks with the sugar until well blended.

3 When the cream is about to reach boiling point, remove from the heat. Remove the vanilla pod, if used, and scrape out the little black seeds. Return the seeds to the cream. Pour the cream over the egg yolk mixture and stir well.

4 Return the egg and cream to the pan and place in another pan filled with boiling water (or use a double saucepan). Cook the custard until thick, stirring continuously.

5 When the custard is ready, place a few raspberries at the bottom of 4 ramekins or other serving dishes, sprinkle with some of the crushed amaretti, then pour over the warm custard. Sprinkle with the remaining amaretti, leave to stand for 5–10 minutes and serve.

NOTE: If prepared the day before, leave to chill in the refrigerator and the custard will set. You can then top the dessert with a thin layer of caramel.

STRAWBERRY & PEACH FRUIT SALAD IN RED WINE

Strawberries and red wine can be a surprising combination: make sure the berries are ripe and perfumed and the red wine fruity.

> 300 ml/10 fl.oz red wine
> 3 cloves, crushed
> 3 cardamom pods, crushed
> 1–2 tablespoons caster sugar
> 170 g/6 oz strawberries, hulled & halved
> juice of 1 lemon
> 3 peaches, peeled, stoned & sliced

1 Heat one-third of the wine in a small pan with the cloves, cardamom and sugar. Simmer for a couple of minutes.

2 In a bowl mix the remaining wine with the lemon juice and strain into the spiced, cooked wine.

3 Add the prepared fruit and serve. This dish can also be served chilled.

ZABAGLIONE

Zabaglione is a great invention! A terrific pick-me-up if you do not have a problem with cholesterol. When you have mastered the technique, experiment with different wines.

4 egg yolks
4 tablespoons caster sugar
4 tablespoons Marsala wine
3–4 tablespoons sweet white wine

1   Set a mixing bowl over a pan of boiling water. In the bowl, vigorously whisk the egg yolks with the sugar over a medium heat until the mixture begins to thicken and lighten. It is important that the heat under the bowl is not too high or the mixture will curdle.

2   Whisk in the Marsala and white wine in small quantities at regular intervals until both have been incorporated (the mixture should be thick and velvety, not frothy). Then pour into glasses and serve with sponge fingers or fresh strawberries, ripe apricots and figs to dip in.

NOTE: Zabaglione can also be served cold. After preparing it as instructed above, place the hot mixing bowl over ice and keep stirring or lightly whisking until the zabaglione is completely cold. Use as it is or as a sauce.

APRICOT & MARSALA FOOL

It is very important that the apricots are ripe. If you cannot find ripe ones, try cooking them instead (see note below).

6 very ripe apricots, stoned
1 tablespoon icing sugar
2 tablespoons Marsala wine
300 ml/10 fl.oz double cream
1 tablespoon toasted flaked almonds

1   Blend the apricots, icing sugar and Marsala in a liquidizer.

2   Whip the cream in a bowl until it holds its shape, then fold in the apricot mixture.

3   Spoon into serving glasses or ramekins, sprinkle with the almonds and serve.

NOTE: To cook unripe apricots, stone and quarter them, add 2–3 tablespoons of water, a couple of tablespoons of icing sugar and a squeeze of lemon and cook over a low heat until the apricots are soft and translucent. Then liquidize, leave to cool and proceed from Step 2 of the recipe.

TOFFEE BAKED APPLES

I doubt if Marsala wine features in many toffee recipes, but I do not feel it is out of place here. John Woodhouse first produced it in Sicily in the late eighteenth century and it is said to have invigorated Nelson and his royal navy!

4 tablespoons soft brown sugar
100 g / 4 oz unsalted butter
2 tablespoons golden syrup
1 tablespoon treacle
2 tablespoons rum or Marsala wine
450 ml / 15 fl.oz double cream
4 Bramley apples, halved horizontally
25 g / 1 oz toasted flaked almonds

1   Melt the sugar with the butter, golden syrup and treacle in a flameproof dish over a low heat. When the mixture is well blended and starts to bubble, add the rum or Marsala and 300 ml/10 fl.oz of the cream. Mix well and bring to the boil.

2   Remove the dish from the heat and place the apples in it, cut side down. Bake in a pre-heated oven at 220°C/425°F/Gas Mark 7 for 8–10 minutes.

3   Remove the apples from the oven and reassemble them. Pour over the cooking juices and the remaining cream. Sprinkle with the almonds and enjoy!

WARM BERRIES ON TOASTED PANETTONE WITH CLOTTED CREAM

Throughout the Christmas season hundreds of panettoni dangle from the ceilings and shelves of most Italian delicatessens. This traditional cake is in effect a light bread dough enriched with butter, candied peel and sultanas. At breakfast or teatime try toasting left-over slices spread with honey.

75 g / 3 oz redcurrant jelly
juice of 1 lemon
1–2 tablespoons brandy
4 slices of panettone
75 g / 3 oz strawberries, hulled & halved
75 g / 3 oz blueberries, washed & drained
75 g / 3 oz blackberries, washed & drained
75 g / 3 oz raspberries, washed & drained
icing sugar for dusting
4 tablespoons clotted cream

1   Gently melt the redcurrant jelly with the lemon juice and brandy in a frying pan.

2   Meanwhile, toast the panettone slices on both sides and keep warm.

3   When the jelly has melted and is well blended with the other ingredients, add all the berries and toss gently, coating the fruit with the hot syrupy mixture.

4   Place the toasted panettone on serving plates, spoon on the hot fruit and dust with icing sugar. Serve with a dollop of clotted cream.

WARM POACHED PEARS IN WINE WITH MASCARPONE

My grandfather used to poach small rust-skinned pears in red wine every autumn and winter. The pears were allowed to cool in the poaching liquid then kept in jars in the pantry: each pear a delicious treat!

4 firm conference pears
1 cinnamon stick
1 vanilla pod, split in half lengthways
3 tablespoons caster sugar
zest of ½ orange
zest of ½ lemon
900 ml / 1½ pints red wine
150 g / 5 oz mascarpone cheese

1 Peel, halve and remove the pips from the pears and place in a pan where they will fit tightly. Add the cinnamon, the vanilla pod, the sugar and the citrus zest and cover with the wine. Weight the pears down with a plate, so that they will not float as the juices simmer, bring gently to the boil, then simmer for 10–15 minutes.

2 Remove the plate, carefully take out the pears and keep them warm. Turn the heat up and boil the juices until they have reduced by half.

3 Arrange the pears on serving plates, drizzle on some of the reduced poaching liquid, and accompany with a spoonful of mascarpone. Delicious with cantuccini biscuits (Tuscan almond biscuits).

BAKED PEACHES WITH MACAROON FILLING

Ripe juicy peaches are delicious on their own, but this way they are even better. Try to find white peaches at the end of spring which are delicate in flavour and beautifully perfumed.

4 peaches, halved & stones removed
1 teaspoon amaretto liqueur
6 macaroons or amaretti biscuits, crushed
1 tablespoon ground almonds
50 g / 2 oz unsalted butter

1 With a spoon scoop out a little flesh from the centre of each peach half and gently mash it.

2 In a bowl mix the peach flesh with the liqueur, the macaroons or amaretti and the ground almonds, then spoon back into the peaches.

3 Grease an ovenproof dish with a little of the butter. Arrange the stuffed peach halves in it and dot with the remaining butter.

4 Bake in a pre-heated oven at 220°C/425°F/Gas Mark 7 for about 15 minutes until the peaches are golden-brown and heated through.

5 Serve hot with a little cold zabaglione (page 84) or some double cream.

DATE, SULTANA & ALMOND FILO PARCELS WITH VANILLA ICE-CREAM

Crispy pastry, luxurious filling – even if you have never used filo pastry you must try this recipe!

1 tablespoon water
1 tablespoon brandy
grated rind of ½ orange
2 tablespoons sultanas
12 fresh, ripe dates, stoned & thinly sliced
75 g / 3 oz almonds, roasted & fairly finely chopped
6 sheets of filo pastry
100 g / 4 oz unsalted butter, melted
icing sugar for dusting
4 scoops vanilla ice-cream

1. Heat the water with the brandy and orange rind in a saucepan. Add the sultanas and simmer for 4–5 minutes, then drain off excess juices and leave to cool.

2. In a bowl mix together the dates, almonds and cooled sultanas. Set aside.

3. With a pastry brush, brush one half of one sheet of filo pastry with the melted butter. Fold the unbuttered half over the buttered one, then brush again with butter. Cut the folded, twice-buttered sheet of pastry in half lengthways.

4. Place a spoonful of the date mixture at the base of each strip of pastry. Gently fold in the edges of each strip, butter lightly, then roll the pastry to make a neat barrel-shaped parcel.

5. Proceed from Step 3 until all the pastry and the filling are used up. Then place the parcels on a baking tray and bake in a pre-heated oven at 220°C/425°F/Gas Mark 7 for about 8–10 minutes or until golden-brown.

7. When the parcels are ready, remove from the oven and place on serving dishes. Dust with icing sugar and serve with the vanilla ice-cream. SCRUMMY!

BANANA, APPLE & CHOCOLATE CRUMBLE

Crumble: what a great invention! Try different combinations throughout the seasons – peach and apricot, raspberry and apple, pear and dried figs, apple, orange and sultanas. A meal in themselves!

2 large bananas, peeled & sliced
2 medium Bramley apples, peeled, cored & cut into chunks
1 tablespoon rum
juice of ½ lemon
1 tablespoon icing sugar plus extra for dusting
2 tablespoons grated dark chocolate

For the crumble
175 g / 6 oz plain flour
150 g / 5 oz cold unsalted butter, cut into cubes
50 g / 2 oz ground hazelnuts
50 g / 2 oz soft brown sugar

1 In a bowl mix the bananas and apples with the rum, lemon juice and icing sugar, then pack tightly into an ovenproof dish, sprinkle with the grated chocolate and set aside.

2 Make the crumble: place the flour in a food processor and activate the blade, then add the butter a piece at a time. Toss the mixture in a bowl and fold in the hazelnuts and sugar.

3 Spoon the crumble on to the fruit, covering the entire surface neatly and pressing the mixture on to the fruit.

4 Bake in a pre-heated oven at 220°C/425°F/Gas Mark 7 for 15–20 minutes (the juices should bubble around the edges and the topping should be golden-brown).

5 Serve with pouring cream or ice-cream.

BLUEBERRY PANCAKES WITH CRÈME FRAÎCHE

Use fresh fruit, not frozen or tinned, not just for better flavour but also because the pancakes will become too wet otherwise.

100 g / 4 oz plain flour
1 tablespoon caster sugar
2 tablespoons double cream
2 eggs, separated
grated rind of 1 lemon
225 ml / 8 fl.oz milk
unsalted butter
1 punnet of fresh blueberries, washed & drained
4–6 tablespoons maple syrup
4 tablespoons crème fraîche

1   Sift the flour into a bowl, mix in the sugar and make a well in the centre.

2   In a separate bowl mix the double cream, egg yolks, lemon rind and milk. Pour into the well in the flour and mix thoroughly, using a small whisk or a wooden spoon, to make a smooth batter.

4   Whisk the egg whites until stiff. Gently spoon a third of them into the flour to loosen the texture, then fold in the rest.

5   Melt a small knob of butter in a 15-cm/6-in frying pan. Pour in one-quarter of the batter (the pancake should not be more than 1 cm/½ in thick) and sprinkle with some blueberries. When small bubbles begin to break on the surface, flip the pancake over and cook for another minute or two. Slide on to a warm serving plate, drizzle with maple syrup and keep warm.

6   Make 3 more pancakes with the remaining batter in the same way, then serve with a dollop of crème fraîche: DELICIOUS!

CHOCOLATE & HAZELNUT TRUFFLE CUPS

I have always been fond of hazelnuts, which mix with chocolate very well. If you ever find yourself in Turin, try Gianduiotti, oddly shaped hazelnut chocolates that are, in my opinion, the best combination of the two ingredients.

170 g / 6 oz dark chocolate
2–3 tablespoons rum or brandy
100 g / 4 oz hazelnuts, roasted, skins removed & roughly chopped
2 egg whites
2 tablespoons caster sugar
300 ml / 10 fl.oz double cream

1 Melt the chocolate with the rum or brandy and the hazelnuts in a bowl over a pan of simmering water. When melted, remove from the heat and cool, stirring occasionally until lukewarm.

2 Whisk the egg whites until they hold their shape, then add the sugar and whisk until stiff. Set aside.

3 Whisk the double cream until thick.

4 Fold the egg whites into the chocolate mixture and mix well, then fold in the cream. Spoon into serving cups, chill for 10 minutes and serve.

Index